# Suffering And Song

---

## Lives Of Hymn Writers

---

# Julia Ann Flora

*With God's blessing,*
*Julie Flora*

***Fairway Press***
***A Division of CSS Publishing***
***Lima, Ohio***

SUFFERING AND SONG

Library of Congress Catalog Card Number: 95-61124

ISBN 0-7880-0616-9
PRINTED IN U.S.A.

*To the Memory
of My Parents
Weir E. Tritch
and
Herma S. Tritch*

# Table Of Contents

# Foreword

Contemporary Christians too often forget that every hymn in every hymnbook was new at one time, and that every hymn has a unique story. Drawing on years of personal interest and research in Christian hymnody, Julie Flora has authored an excellent resource for the general church. Knowing the stories that birthed the hymns can greatly assist planners and leaders of Christian worship.

We also recommend Julie Flora's book
- as an elective course for short term study groups and Sunday School classes;
- a resource for teachers of older children and youth, especially for confirmation classes;
- a personal study guide for those who turn to hymns for prayer and meditation.

Several months after Mary Lou's father was tragically killed in an auto accident, her mother shared this with the family: "It was the strength and comfort I received from the hymns I had memorized that kept me company through those long nights and days of adjustment."

This is why Martin Luther once remarked that next to the Bible his hymnal was the most important book in his library. And this is why *Suffering and Song*, a well written, user-friendly book, is needed to bring musical balance, appreciation and inspiration to the church today.

James K. and Mary Lou Wagner

Dr. James K. Wagner is Pastor of Fairview United Methodist Church, Dayton, Ohio, and former Director of the Upper Room Healing Ministries. Mary Lou Wagner is an accomplished musician and experienced teacher.

# Introduction

All my life I have sung the great hymns of Christian faith. In childhood my parents took me to church every week. By fifth grade I was playing the piano for a children's worship service. In college I began to learn more about hymnody in classes taught by composer Eunice Lea Kettering. For the last eight years I have researched the lives of hymn writers. After hearing me tell some of these stories, a number of people have asked me to put them into permanent form.

What is unique about this book compared to other collections of hymn backgrounds? One difference is the length of these chapters. I have collected all the material I can find on each writer, some having more information available than others. Because of this the chapters vary in length, while some other books keep them all about the same. Further, I have not broken up the leading writers' lives, separating the pieces among various hymns they wrote. Instead, in each chapter I have included stories of all their most popular hymns. Therefore, these are basically biographies of the writers.

Second, in the interest of historical progression I have arranged the chapters in each section in chronological order. They are set according to the writers' lives and the date of their hymn's writing or first printing. The Appendix is a time-line or short history of hymnology. As is explained there concerning the twentieth century, it is difficult to know what hymns, of the many new ones we have, will last in popularity. Therefore, this collection emphasizes the rich heritage we share from the past.

Third, due to length and space I have not included the musicians' lives for all of the hymns. The word "hymn" refers to the text, not the music. The tune, along with an arrangement of the harmony, is just as important as the words. It becomes complicated, however, when there are many people involved with one hymn. Along with the text's author, for example, there may be at times a translator, a composer of the tune, and an arranger who harmonized a famous melody into four parts for congregational singing. So this book will concentrate on the words of the hymns and the lives of their authors.

Fourth, these chapters grew out of a Sunday school class I taught using these hymns, their stories and Scripture references related to the texts. I have arranged the material so it can be presented once each week for three quarters, or two to three hymns weekly for one quarter. The Scripture references are taken from Donald A. Spencer's 1993 *Hymn and Scripture Selection Guide* and can assist in both personal study and group discussion.

I am grateful to two people who have been my writing teachers through the years: the Reverend Richard C. Winfield, Editor of Publications for the Brethren Church, and my husband, Dr. Jerry R. Flora, Professor of Theology and Spiritual Formation at Ashland Theological Seminary. I also wish to thank two others on the Ashland Seminary faculty: my professor of hymnology, Dr. Ronald L. Sprunger, and Dr. David W. Baker, who helped with the prospectus for the book.

The hymns we sing which help us along our Christian journey become more meaningful as we come to know about the authors who gave them birth. "They learn in suffering what they teach in song" (Percy B. Shelley). In suffering and song they have written about the God of creation, the Christ of redemption, and our consecration to God's work and worship.

Julie Flora
Ashland, Ohio

10

# A Mighty Fortress Is Our God

## *Martin Luther (1483-1546)*

---

*A mighty fortress is our God, a bulwark never failing;*
*our helper he amid the flood of mortal ills prevailing.*
*For still our ancient foe doth seek to work us woe;*
*his craft and power are great, and armed with cruel hate,*
*    on earth is not his equal.*

*Did we in our own strength confide, our striving would*
*    be losing,*
*were not the right man on our side, the man of God's*
*    own choosing.*
*Dost ask who that may be? Christ Jesus, it is he;*
*Lord Sabaoth, his name, from age to age the same, and*
*    he must win the battle.*

*And though this world, with devils filled, should threat-*
*    en to undo us,*
*we will not fear, for God hath willed his truth to triumph*
*    through us.*
*The Prince of Darkness grim, we tremble not for him;*
*his rage we can endure, for lo, his doom is sure; one lit-*
*    tle word shall fell him.*

*That word above all earthly powers, no thanks to them,*
*    abideth;*
*the Spirit and the gifts are ours, thro' him who with us*
*    sideth.*
*Let goods and kindred go, this mortal life also;*
*the body they may kill; God's truth abideth still; his king-*
*    dom is forever.*

Martin Luther was born in Eisleben, Germany, in 1483. He was raised in a modest environment with a gentle mother and a very strict father. Music was always an important part of his life for he had a remarkable singing voice along with talent for the flute and lute. He liked to stand at the windows of the wealthy and sing for money, which was a custom of the day. One woman was so impressed when she heard him that she invited him to stay in her home during his school years.

Hymns seemed almost like a miniature Bible to Luther after he became an Augustinian monk, teaching philosophy and theology at the University of Wittenberg. He said that "after theology, there is nothing that can be placed on a level with music. Now we need to remove the hymn singing from the domain of monks and priests and set the laity to singing. By the singing of hymns the laity can publicly express their love to the almighty God."

Luther was the originator of congregational singing, which finally resulted in the publication during four centuries of 100,000 German hymns. He said that "Music is a gift and grace of God . . . . It drives out the Devil and makes people cheerful. The Devil, the originator of sorrowful anxieties and restless troubles, flees before the sound of music almost as much as before the Word of God. I would allow no one to preach or teach God's people without a proper knowledge of the use and power of sacred song."

In 1520 Luther was excommunicated from the Catholic Church. In 1524, just seven years after his famous "Ninety-five Theses" were nailed to the church door at Wittenberg, his first hymn book was published containing eight hymns, four of which were by Luther himself.

Luther was led to write hymns when he learned that two young people from Brussels were burned at the stake for their belief in the reformed faith. In honor of these two martyrs he wrote his hymn that was to become one of the most effective promoters for the advancement of the Reformation.

All of Germany was soon singing "A Mighty Fortress Is Our God." A Spanish monk, Thomas a Jesu, noted, "It is surprising how those hymns spread Lutheranism. Written in German, they literally flew out of Luther's study, landing in homes, in places of work and were sung in the markets, in the street, and on the field."

Martin Luther died in 1546. Around the castle church where he is buried a beautiful mosaic forms the words of this great reformation hymn. With its outstanding tune, also by Luther, it quickly spread over all Germany and became the favorite hymn for national days, church anniversaries, and various other occasions.

This hymn has become one of the standard hymns of the American church. By 1900 there were 80 translations in 53 languages.

"A Mighty Fortress Is Our God" is a paraphrase of the 46th Psalm. It is a spiritual tonic for those who are discouraged with life. It speaks, for instance, of conflict with "the prince of darkness grim," difficulties like a "flood of mortal ills," or the "world with devils filled," threatening "to undo us." But we hear Luther's confidence in the one "of God's own choosing ... from age to age the same," so Jesus Christ "must win the battle." The first line of the hymn is inscribed on the tomb of this great reformer from Germany.

Scripture References: Ps. 46; Deut. 33:27; 2 Sam. 22:2-4; Ps. 59:16-17; 73:26; 91:2; 94:22; 118:6, 8; Isa. 26:4; 40:28-29; Heb. 2:14-17; 6:13-19; 13:6

# If Thou But Suffer God To Guide Thee

## George Neumark (1621-1681)

*If thou but suffer God to guide thee,*
*and hope in God through all thy ways,*
*God will give strength, whate'er betide thee,*
*and bear thee through the evil days.*
*Who trusts in God's unchanging love*
*builds on the rock that naught can move.*

*Only be still, and wait God's leisure*
*in cheerful hope, with heart content*
*to take whate'er thy Maker's pleasure*
*and all-discerning love hath sent;*
*we know our inmost wants are known,*
*for we are called to be God's own.*

*Sing, pray, and keep God's ways unswerving;*
*so do thine own part faithfully,*
*and trust God's word; though undeserving,*
*thou yet shalt find it true for thee.*
*God never yet forsook at need*
*the soul that trusted God indeed.*

George Neumark was born in Thuringia, March 16, 1621. In 1641 he was on his way to the university in Konigsberg, East Prussia. He wanted to enroll there since it was the only university left in that country that was not closed due to the Thirty Years' War. He was traveling with a caravan of merchants hoping to be safe from robbers. But even the caravan was attacked and the robbers took everything Neumark had, including most of his money. They left a prayer book and a little money he had sewn into his clothes. Due to the robbery it was impossible for him to enter the university. For a long time he searched for work, found nothing and finally became destitute.

In one town he became friends with a Lutheran pastor who helped him find work. A judge employed Mr. Neumark as a tutor for his family. After all his earlier problems, the tutoring job with its security brought him much joy. He later wrote about this special time. The job "coming suddenly, as if it had fallen from heaven, greatly rejoiced me, and on that day I composed to the honor of my beloved Lord the hymn."

He saved his money and after two years he enrolled in the university, studying law and poetry. He later became court librarian, registrar, and poet for Duke Wilhelm II at Thuringia, as well as being responsible for the Ducal Archives.

Many of his hymns were born out of suffering and sorrow. George Neumark died July 18, 1681, in Weimar. Only this hymn of the 34 he wrote has survived and been popular. It is based on Psalm 55:22, which reads, "Cast your burden on the Lord, and he will sustain you." The first title given for the text was "A Song of Comfort." The word "suffer" in the first line means to "allow" or "let" God govern or control one's life. The words of the last stanza show author Neumark's great confidence in God when he declares, "God never yet forsook at need the soul that trusted God indeed."

Scripture References: Deut. 31:8; Ps. 9:10; 25:4-10; 118:14; Prov. 3:5-6; Isa. 58:11; Phil. 4:19

# Doxology

## *Thomas Ken (1637-1711)*

---

*Praise God, from whom all blessings flow;*
*praise him, all creatures here below;*
*praise him above, ye heavenly host;*
*praise Father, Son, and Holy Ghost.*

The word "doxology" comes from two Greek words. One of the words means "to speak," and the other means "glory." The lines which we call the Doxology were the closing stanza of three different hymns that the author, Thomas Ken, wrote for the devotions of students at Winchester College, England.

Thomas Ken was born in Hertfordshire, England, in 1637, orphaned early in his life, and reared by a sister. He became a conscientious, godly man who was a scholar and outstanding preacher. The king, Charles II, admired him so much that in 1679 he appointed him as Chaplain to Princess Mary and later to himself. While Ken filled this position he tried to convert the king to a deeper Christianity. Ken was sometimes firm with the king and did not always obey him.

Once Charles was intending to visit the Reverend Ken at Winchester Cathedral and wanted his mistress to stay in Ken's house. Ken was so upset about it that he tried to keep it from happening. He soon started repairs on the house and, in the process, removed the roof. Therefore the king had to make other arrangements, since Ken's house was without a roof.

At times, after the king had been "living it up" he would say, "Now I must go and hear good Bishop Ken tell me my faults.'' We are not sure if he ever changed the king, but Ken was warned that he could lose his head if he wasn't careful. Someone has said, ''His inflexibility in maintaining what he believed to be right, and his courage in reproving kings where it was necessary, made him many and powerful enemies.'' Because of his aggressiveness he lost his office, but in sympathy Queen Anne allotted him 200 pounds yearly.

The rest of Thomas Ken's days were lived quietly, away from the public eye. He died in 1711 at age 74 and was buried at a simple service in a modest tomb. For a fitting eulogy of this deeply Christian man, hymnists have written, ''He approached as near as infirmity permits to the ideal perfection of Christian virtue.''

This text is the most widely used of all the doxologies in the English language. It is sung almost every Sunday in all churches and on many other special occasions to give expression of great joy, praise, and gratitude.

The tune most used with these words is called OLD HUNDREDTH and comes from Louis Bourgeois, music director at John Calvin's St. Peter's Church in Geneva from 1545 until 1557. For 15 years he was editor for the music of Calvin's psalters. He composed and arranged tunes to fit the poetic versions of the Psalms. This tune was first composed in 1557 for a hymn on Psalm 134, but it was used more for another hymn, ''All People That On Earth Do Dwell.''

When the Doxology was written in the early 1700s, congregations were still using the metrical Psalms. They moved words around in the Psalms to put them into rhythm, thus having a pattern and a beat that the older way of chanting the Psalms did not have. Chants had been used in the Catholic Church where only the clergy sang, but Calvin wanted the people to sing pure Scripture.

The first collection of metrical Psalms was published in 1562 and used from then on. Many people were illiterate, so one person would read the first line and the others would sing it very slowly. Then the second line would be read and sung, and so on until the hymn was completed. The organ would play interludes during the reading. This was called "lining the hymn." The metrical Psalms were being used until Isaac Watts and others started writing their own original poems which were added to the Psalm hymns. The Psalm tunes of Bourgeois put with Scripture laid the foundation for English hymnody.

Three stories will illustrate specific occasions when the Doxology was sung. The first occurred during a cotton famine in Lancashire, England. Unemployment was serious. When a wagonload of cotton finally arrived, the men unharnessed the horse, pulled the wagonload of cotton through the streets, and with tears of joy sang this hymn of praise.

In 1936, newspapers in Canada and the United States showed headlines of an abandoned mine disaster in Nova Scotia. Three men, a physician, a lawyer and a guide, had been exploring their new purchase. There was a cave-in which cut off all means of escape. Rescue squads lowered a pipe in which they were sent food and by which they could communicate. When the rescuers finally reached them after ten days, they found one man dead. They were saddened by the death, but very thankful for the two lives saved. All the people involved at the cave joined in singing the Doxology.

Finally, Charles Wesley, the eighteenth century English preacher and hymn writer, was preaching on the second floor of a dilapidated old house in Leeds, when the floor gave way with a crash. The whole congregation of 100 people fell to a room below. Several were injured while dust and plaster covered everyone, but no lives were lost. Wesley called out, "The Lord is with us! Let us sing 'Praise God, From Whom All Blessings Flow.'" It remains today the most universal hymn of praise sung in our churches.

Spiritual References: Ps. 103:2-22; 148:1-2, 11-13; 150:1-2, 6; Matt. 28:19; 1 Cor. 8:5-6; 2 Cor. 13:14; Jude 20-21

# O God, Our Help In Ages Past

## Isaac Watts (1674-1748)

*O God, our help in ages past,*
*our hope for years to come,*
*our shelter from the stormy blast,*
*and our eternal home!*

*Under the shadow of thy throne,*
*still may we dwell secure;*
*sufficient is thine arm alone,*
*and our defense is sure.*

*Before the hills in order stood,*
*or earth received her frame,*
*from everlasting, thou art God,*
*to endless years the same.*

*A thousand ages, in thy sight,*
*are like an evening gone;*
*short as the watch that ends the night,*
*before the rising sun.*

*Time, like an ever rolling stream,*
*bears all who breathe away;*
*they fly forgotten, as a dream*
*dies at the opening day.*

*O God, our help in ages past,*
*our hope for years to come;*
*be thou our guide while life shall last,*
*and our eternal home.*

In the 1500s Martin Luther's reformation brought hymn singing into Protestant congregations whereas in the Roman Catholic Church there were clergy choirs but no congregational singing. Neither was the Bible used by the lay people. The Psalms of David, considered the song book of the Bible, were used in chant form (without rhyme or meter).

In 1562 a song book was published by Sternhold and Hopkins called the "metrical psalter." The Psalms were translated from the Hebrew, their original language, to English and arranged in poetic form with rhyme and meter. Another such book was the Bay Psalm Book printed in America in 1640. At this time congregations sang only tunes (the melody), not parts (harmony).

In the 1700s many changes were made in the field of music by Isaac Watts, who is called the "father of hymnody." He contributed greatly to church worship through his nearly 700 hymns. For several years worshipers in England sang only the hymns Watts wrote.

This outstanding churchman was born on July 17, 1674, in Southampton, England, the oldest of nine children. His father was a deacon in the Bar Congregational Church in Southampton. When Isaac was a baby, his mother took him to a prison to visit his father, who had been taken there for his nonconformity to the established laws of the Anglican Church. Isaac took his schooling at a nonconformist academy instead of the Anglican school.

Isaac always had a spiritual nature. When he was only seven years old he wrote an acrostic, with the beginning letters spelling out his name.

I  am a vile, polluted lump of earth.
S  o I've continued ever since my birth.
A  s sure this monster, Satan, will deceive me.
C  ome therefore, Lord, from Satan's claws relieve me.
W  ash me in Thy blood, O Christ,
A  nd grace divine impart.
T  hen search and try the corners of my heart.
T  hat I in all things may be fit to do
S  ervice to Thee, and Thy praise, too.

As Isaac grew older people noticed that he was very bright. He had an annoying habit of rhyming much of the time, even everyday conversation. One day when he was scolded by his irritated father for rhyming again, he blurted out, "Oh, Father, do some pity take and I will no more verse make." Another time the Watts family were having devotions. During his father's prayer, Isaac just happened to glance up and see a mouse running up a bell rope beside the fireplace. At the close of the prayer he offered his next little rhyme: "A mouse, for want of better stairs, ran up a rope to say his prayers."

When Watts was about 18, he became very dissatisfied with the Psalm singing in his father's church. After Isaac criticized it one Sunday, his father said, "Well then, young man, why don't you give us something better to sing?" The boy took his father's challenge and by the next service he had written his first hymn. When he presented it to the congregation, they liked it. He continued to write a hymn for each Sunday until he had over 200 texts. Sometimes he paraphrased the Psalms or rewrote them in his own words. In 1707 he published a book called *Hymns and Spiritual Songs* including 210 original hymns as well as the paraphrases of the Psalms. He wanted more New Testament themes. He thought that it would be the way the Psalmist David would have sung them if he had lived in the days of Christianity.

In the preface to his book *Hymns and Spiritual Songs* Watts wrote, "While we sing the praises of God in His church, we are employed in that part of worship which of all others is the nearest akin to heaven; and 'tis pity that this of all others should be performed the worst upon earth ...."

At that time churches would parcel-out or line-out hymns, meaning that one leader would sing or say a line and the congregation would repeat it. This took a long time and incomplete sentences were left hanging, which made it very difficult to understand. He wanted complete stanzas sung at one time. This new way was called "regular singing."

Concerning his work Watts wrote, "It was not my design to exalt myself to the rank and glory of poets, but I was ambitious to be a servant to the churches and a helper to the joy of the Christian.'' His other writing included essays, discussions on psychology, three volumes of sermons, catechisms, 29 treatises on theology, textbooks on logic, and others. His prolific writing had a large influence on the thinking of his time. John and Charles Wesley of the Methodists were apparently familiar with the hymns of Watts. In the early 1730s their Holy Club of Oxford was using his psalms and hymns before Charles Wesley began to write hymns.

Isaac Watts, who was only five feet tall and ill much of his life, died in 1748 at the age of 74. His monument was placed in Westminster Abbey, the highest honor for the English. At least twenty of his hymns are world famous. Some of them are: ''Jesus Shall Reign,'' ''Joy to the World,'' and ''When I Survey the Wondrous Cross.''

The tune for ''O God, Our Help in Ages Past'' is named ST. ANNE. It was composed by William Croft in 1708. He had a Doctor of Music Degree from Oxford University and was organist in St. Anne's Church, Soho, London, during the reign of Queen Anne.

The hymn was first published in 1719 in Watts' book *Psalms of David*. The title first was ''Man Frail and God Eternal.'' Later it became ''*Our* God, Our Help ....'' But reformer John Wesley changed it to ''*O* God, Our Help ....'' It is a paraphrase of Psalm 90, which reads, ''Lord, you have been our dwelling place in all generations. Before the mountains were brought forth, or ever you had formed the earth and the world, from everlasting to everlasting you are God.'' Like the Psalm, it is a majestic, serene, deep, moving hymn of faith.

Scripture References: Ps. 33:20; 46:1; 48:14, 91:1-2; Isa. 26:4; Lam. 5:19; 2 Thess. 3:3.

# Guide Me,
# O Thou Great Jehovah

## *William Williams (1717-1791)*

---

*Guide me, O thou great Jehovah, pilgrim through this
    barren land.
I am weak, but thou art mighty; hold me with thy power-
    ful hand.
Bread of heaven, bread of heaven,
feed me till I want no more;
feed me till I want no more.*

*Open now the crystal fountain, whence the healing stream
    doth flow;
let the fire and cloudy pillar lead me all my journey
    through.
Strong deliverer, strong deliverer,
be thou still my strength and shield;
be thou still my strength and shield.*

*When I tread the verge of Jordan, bid my anxious fears
    subside;
death of death and hell's destruction, land me safe on
    Canaan's side.
Songs of praises, songs of praises,
I will ever give to thee;
I will ever give to thee.*

William Williams was the son of a prominent farmer in
Wales. For his career he first chose the medical profession.
But while he was preparing to be a doctor, his life was com-
pletely changed one Sunday morning.

As he was walking he heard church bells. Following the sound, he was led into a church. The service seemed cold and dull to him. As he left the church he noticed many people standing around waiting for something. Soon a tall man climbed onto a flat tombstone as he began to speak (a custom of that time and place). He was a well-known preacher who emphasized individual personal experience as essential to a relationship with Christ. He was part of a renewal movement within the churches of Great Britain at that time led by the Wesleys.

Williams was so impressed by what he heard that he left the Anglican Church where he had been a pastor for three years and joined the Wesleys, who were being called Methodists. During 43 years of ministry he traveled nearly 100,000 miles on horseback, preaching and singing. He became known as the "sweet singer of Wales." This hymn is the best known of his nearly 800 hymns. His wife was a gifted singer also and accompanied him on his itinerant preaching missions. At times it was dangerous. Once a local gang attacked and beat him almost to death for his preaching.

The Welsh people are known for their love of music. They used Williams' hymns to learn to read. Welsh miners customarily sang on their way to work in the coal pits. Sometimes in the great spiritual awakenings which came to Wales, music became more effective than preaching. Their pastors were not offended by spontaneous outbursts of congregational song.

This prayer for guidance has been translated into 75 different languages. It recalls Biblical incidents through the desert from Egypt to the promised land of Canaan. One joy of the Christian life is consciousness that God is with us each moment, guiding, protecting, and providing. So we sing with our sisters and brothers in Wales, "Songs of praises, songs of praises I will ever give to thee."

Scripture References: Ps. 23; 28:7; 48:14; 73:24; Phil. 4:19
St. 1   Exod. 16:4, 18; Deut. 9:29
St. 2   Exod. 13:21-22; 2 Sam. 22:2
St. 3   Josh. 3:17; Ps. 27:4-6; Rev. 1:18; 7:9-17

24

# Glorious Things Of Thee Are Spoken

## John Newton (1725-1807)

---

*Glorious things of thee are spoken, Zion, city of our God;*
*God, whose word cannot be broken, formed thee for his*
*own abode.*
*On the Rock of Ages founded, what can shake thy sure*
*repose?*
*With salvation's walls surrounded, thou mayst smile at*
*all thy foes.*

*See, the streams of living waters, springing from eternal*
*love,*
*well supply thy sons and daughters, and all fear of want*
*remove.*
*Who can faint while such a river ever will their thirst*
*assuage?*
*Grace which like the Lord, the giver, never fails from age*
*to age.*

*Round each habitation hovering, see the cloud and fire*
*appear*
*for a glory and a covering, showing that the Lord is near!*
*Thus deriving from our banner light by night and shade*
*by day,*
*safe we feed upon the manna which God gives us when*
*we pray.*

*Blest inhabitants of Zion, washed in our Redeemer's*
*blood;*
*Jesus, whom our souls rely on, makes us monarchs,*
*priests to God.*
*Us, by his great love, he raises, rulers over self to reign,*
*and as priests his solemn praises we for thankful offer-*
*ing bring.*

John Newton lived a dramatic life during the eighteenth century. As a small child in England he learned about the Bible from his mother, but she died when he was only seven. At a young age he could recite much of the Bible and many hymns by Isaac Watts. His mother had prayed that he would become a minister, and her prayers were finally answered.

For two years following his mother's death he attended school. His father, who was in the British Navy, then took John with him sailing the seas. He became wild and blasphemous during his 18 years as a sailor. Six of those years he was captain of a slave ship.

Once he was allowed to visit some of his mother's relatives. While there he fell in love with Mary Catlett, whom he later married. Instead of going on to Jamaica as his father instructed, he missed the boat on purpose and stayed with Mary. In his anger his father threatened to disown him as he had done many times before.

There were several influences which led to Newton's decision to follow Christ. One was Mary, who was a devout Christian. Another influence was his recovery from a serious fever while in Africa. Also, he served with a godly captain on one of the ships, where he read *The Imitation of Christ* by Thomas a Kempis.

When Newton was 23, while steering a ship through a terrible storm that threatened his life, he began to pray as he turned his life over to Christ. Following this life-changing decision he settled down in Liverpool, England, to nine years of study for the ministry. He was ordained to the ministry and served churches for the next 50 years.

One church was in Olney, Buckinghamshire, famous for its bobbin lace. John and Mary were happy there. For his Bible classes he added new hymns to the ones already in use. With the help of his hymn-writer friend, William Cowper, he published a book in 1779 called *Olney Hymns*. In one English hymn collection of 348 hymns, Newton wrote 283 of them. The most well-known is "Amazing Grace." It has become probably the most popular hymn of our day.

Knowing the hymn stories can be beneficial in defending our Christian faith. For example, a college student studying slavery in a history class was looking at slides of slaves in chains and nets that were "so gross, you could hardly look at them." At the same time the public address system played "Amazing Grace." When the music ended the professor launched into a bitter attack on Christianity, saying that John Newton was a hypocrite because he was the captain of a slave ship.

The student, who didn't know a thing about John Newton, felt that anyone who could write something like "Amazing Grace" had to be a genuine Christian. He spent the night reading about Newton's life and found that Newton had worked to abolish slavery, influencing leaders in the British Empire. The next day the student asked the professor for time to answer the unfair treatment of Christianity. The professor allowed him time in the name of academic freedom, so the student spoke of his findings on Newton. As a result, several other students were impressed by his discovery of Newton's life and drawn toward Christianity.

When Newton was 80 years old and could no longer read his text, he was urged to give up preaching. To that he replied, "What! Shall the old African blasphemer stop while he can speak?" He continued preaching as long as possible. Many times he said, "I remember two things: that I am a great sinner and that Christ is a great Savior." Death for this faithful minister and hymn writer came early in the nineteenth century in 1807.

The tune for "Glorious Things of Thee Are Spoken" was composed by Joseph Haydn (1732-1809), just seven years younger than Newton. It was first performed for the birthday of Austria's emperor. Therefore it was titled "Hymn to the Emperor." For that occasion it had other words appropriate for the celebration.

Haydn was a spiritually devout man who thought of his musical talent as a treasure lent to him by God. His religious nature was extremely joyous. "When I think of God," he said, "my heart dances within me and my music has to dance, too."

This tune was a great favorite of Haydn's. The story is told that when the French were bombarding Vienna in the closing year of his life, Haydn asked to be led to the piano. He played this melody and it was his last musical performance, for his death came five days later. This is one example of a national song (the Austrian National Anthem) which has been taken over by the church.

The sturdy tune matches well the text which comes from Psalm 87:3 where the Psalmist speaks of Jerusalem, "Glorious things are spoken of you, O city of God."

Scripture References: Ps. 9:11; 87:3; Isa. 4:5; 33:20-21
St. 1   Ps. 48:1-2; 87:3; Matt. 7:24-25; 16:18
St. 2   Exod. 17:1-6; John 4:10-14
St. 3   Exod. 13:21-22; 33:14; Num. 9:15

# Holy, Holy, Holy

## *Reginald Heber (1783-1826)*

*Holy, holy, holy! Lord God Almighty!*
*Early in the morning our song shall rise to thee.*
*Holy, holy, holy! Merciful and mighty,*
*God in three persons, blessed Trinity!*

*Holy, holy, holy! All the saints adore thee,*
*casting down their golden crowns around the glassy sea;*
*cherubim and seraphim falling down before thee,*
*which wert, and art, and evermore shalt be.*

*Holy, holy, holy! Though the darkness hide thee,*
*though the eye of sinful man thy glory may not see,*
*only thou art holy; there is none beside thee,*
*perfect in power, in love and purity.*

*Holy, holy, holy! Lord God Almighty!*
*All thy works shall praise thy name, in earth and sky and*
*    sea.*
*Holy, holy, holy! Merciful and mighty,*
*God in three persons, blessed Trinity.*

Reginald Heber was born in Malpas, Cheshire, England, on April 21, 1783. Educated by his father until he was seven, he then attended local school for ten years.

Throughout his life he was courageous. For example, when he was a young boy, the doctor suggested bleeding him to stop his whooping cough. His nurse protested but he held out his arm and said, "Send poor nurse downstairs. I won't stir. Don't hold me."

When he went to school, his money had to be sewn into his pockets so he wouldn't give it all away to the first person in trouble. He was appreciated as an entertainer since he was the center of attraction when he told stories. He was thought of as unselfish and gentle. Someone said of him, "If his heart had no other covering than a glass, its thoughts were so pure, no one need fear to read them."

Reginald Heber received further education at Oxford University where he carried off the prize for Latin verse and other poetry awards. At the age of 26, after ordination to the ministry in the Anglican Church, he became Vicar of Hodnet in western England where he wrote this hymn. He envisioned the importance of good congregational singing. He worked on a welding of sermon, hymns, and liturgy into one unified whole. He began to write hymns appropriate for the various Sundays of the church year and continued all his life to enrich the services of the church.

"Holy, Holy, Holy" has been called the world's greatest hymn by no less an authority than Alfred, Lord Tennyson. The famous Thackeray also paid a high tribute to "the charming poet," as he wrote about Heber being the "happy possessor of all sorts of gifts and accomplishments ... He was the beloved priest in his own home of Hodnet, counseling often at their sick beds at the hazard of his own life; where there was want, the free giver; where there was strife, the peacemaker."

After 16 years at Hodnet, Heber was offered the bishopric of Calcutta. Almost turning it down, he felt it was his duty to accept the offer. He sailed for Calcutta in 1823. His diocese included all of India, Ceylon, and Australia.

He preached only three years in India. His death came suddenly in 1826. There are two versions of how it happened. The first one records that he left his wife and two baby girls in Bombay and started on a journey to Ceylon, Madras, and places in Southern India. One day he plunged into seven feet of water in a pool. Half an hour passed without a sound. When his servant opened the door, his body was seen under the water. The shock of the cold water had caused the bursting of a blood vessel in the brain.

Another version says that he died of a sunstroke after preaching outdoors in India. He was only 43 years old when it happened.

The following year 57 of his hymns were collected and published in a volume titled *Hymns Written and Adapted to the Weekly Service of the Year.* This hymn was written for Trinity Sunday, which is the Sunday after Pentecost.

John Bacchus Dykes (1823-1876) was a clergyman of the Church of England, but he is mostly known as a composer of hymn tunes. Born in Hull and educated at Cambridge, he began his musical career early in life, playing the organ in his grandfather's church when he was only ten and helping to found the University Musical Society at Cambridge while still a student there. After other jobs he became a vicar in Durham where many of his hymn tunes were written. It is said that on Sundays his own family and a few friends frequently spent the evening trying new tunes which Dykes had composed, offering their criticism.

Dykes received his doctor of music degree in 1861 from Durham University. He composed nearly 300 hymn tunes. Hymnals have contained from 20 to 50 of them, a testimony to their singableness.

This hymn contains the doctrine of the Trinity and is a great hymn of adoration.

Scripture References: Exod. 15:11; Deut. 32:3-4; Ps. 30:4; 113:3; 145:8-21; 148; Isa. 6:3; 1 John 5:7; Rev. 4:8-11

# Nearer, My God, To Thee

## Sarah Flower Adams (1805-1848)

*Nearer, my God, to thee, nearer to thee!*
*E'en though it be a cross that raiseth me,*
*still all my song shall be, nearer, my God, to thee;*

*Refrain:*
*nearer, my God, to thee, nearer to thee!*

*Though like the wanderer, the sun gone down,*
*darkness be over me, my rest a stone;*
*yet in my dreams I'd be nearer, my God, to thee;*

*There let the way appear, steps unto heaven;*
*all that thou sendest me, in mercy given;*
*angels to beckon me nearer, my God, to thee;*

*Then, with my waking thoughts bright with thy praise,*
*out of my stony griefs Bethel I'll raise;*
*so by my woes to be nearer, my God, to thee;*

*Or if, on joyful wing cleaving the sky,*
*sun, moon, and stars forgot, upward I fly,*
*still all my song shall be, nearer, my God, to thee;*

Sarah Flower Adams was born in Harlow, England, in 1805. She lost her mother to tuberculosis at age five. Her father, who had been an editor, died when she was 24. She then went to live with the family of a man who edited the magazine *Monthly Repository* and soon she began writing for it.

Three or four years before this hymn was written the dream of her heart came true, which was a dramatic role as Lady Macbeth and the beginning of a career in the theater. At the same time she suddenly developed ill health, causing her to lose what she had worked for in the field of drama.

Inspired by her poet friend, Robert Browning, she turned to writing. She first wrote a long poem called "Vivia Perpetua" on the sufferings of the early Christian martyrs. Vivia's conversion to Christianity symbolized the author's own devotion to the high ideals which inspired her life. She also wrote a Christian catechism titled *The Flock at the Fountain*.

Sarah and her sister, Eliza, worked on hymns together. Eliza composed music for Sarah's texts. They were close friends as well as sisters. When Sarah married and moved to London, Eliza moved to a place close to Sarah's home.

In London they helped their pastor compile a hymnbook, contributing 13 texts and 62 new tunes for the hymnal, which was published in 1841. On one particular occasion her pastor had asked her what he could use as a closing hymn for his sermon about Jacob and Esau. After studying the Biblical account she wrote this hymn. It was published in the 1841 hymnal and introduced in America three years later.

All who knew Mrs. Adams personally spoke of her with enthusiasm. She has been described as a woman of "beauty and attractiveness, delicate and truly feminine, high minded and in her days of health, playful and high-spirited." Other words for her were "charming" and "remarkable."

When her sister, Eliza, became ill with tuberculosis, Sarah nursed her and caught it herself. Sarah died at 43 on August 11, 1848, one and a half years after her sister.

This hymn, starting with the cross, goes through the darkness, like Jacob's dream, to the realization that even this difficult way may be our steps to heaven. If we omit any of the stanzas we break the web of thought. In the fourth stanza the words "out of my stony griefs" refer to the "memorial stone" Jacob used for a pillow at Bethel (Genesis 28:10-22).

We understand that even through our sad times we may be lifted nearer to God. The fifth verse is a joyous climax.

The hymn is a prayer of aspiration in the grayness of our everyday common experience as well as an expression of trust and triumph in God even through difficult times.

Scripture References: Gen. 28:10-21; Ps. 16:8; 73:28; 145:18; Isa. 55:6; Acts 17:27

# To God Be The Glory

## Fanny Crosby (1820-1915)

*To God be the glory, great things he hath done!*
*So loved he the world that he gave us his Son,*
*who yielded his life an atonement for sin,*
*and opened the lifegate that all may go in.*

*Refrain:*
*Praise the Lord, praise the Lord, let the earth hear his*
  *voice!*
*Praise the Lord, praise the Lord, let the people rejoice!*
*O come to the Father thru Jesus the Son,*
*and give him the glory, great things he hath done!*

*O perfect redemption, the purchase of blood,*
*to every believer the promise of God;*
*the vilest offender who truly believes,*
*that moment from Jesus a pardon receives.*

*Great things he hath taught us, great things he hath done,*
*and great our rejoicing thru Jesus the Son;*
*but purer, and higher, and greater will be*
*our wonder, our transport, when Jesus we see.*

The specialist, after making a thorough examination of the little girl's eyes, realized there was nothing more he could do. Her parents were so poor that the doctor's fee had been paid by neighbors and friends. Now, as she and her mother were leaving his office, she heard the doctor say, "Poor little blind girl!" What he could not know was that the small blind girl would turn her handicap into a great blessing for many people.

Frances Jane (Fanny) Crosby was born in New York on March 24, 1820. She caught a cold at the age of six weeks, and a doctor prescribed a mustard poultice for her inflamed eyes. Instead of healing them, it damaged her eyes. By the age of five she was virtually blind, although she could distinguish between day and night.

Cheerful and positive about her blindness, Fanny enjoyed a happy childhood. Three years after that specialist's diagnosis she wrote:

> *Oh, what a happy child I am,*
>    *Although I cannot see!*
> *I am resolved that in this world,*
>    *Contented I will be.*
> *How many blessings I enjoy*
>    *That other people don't.*
> *To weep and sigh because I'm blind,*
>    *I cannot and I won't.*

Commenting on her childhood, she wrote, "I could climb a tree like a squirrel and ride a horse bareback."

While still young she memorized large sections of the Bible including the entire Pentateuch, all four Gospels, many Psalms, all of Proverbs, Ruth and the Song of Solomon. "The Holy Book," she said, "has nurtured my entire life."

At 15 she entered the New York School for the Blind where the teachers gently discouraged her inclination for rhyming. But when a traveling phrenologist proclaimed her a potential poet, she soon became a prodigy of the school. At the end of her training she stayed on, teaching English and history from 1846 to 1858.

One day the school's superintendent found his male secretary, Grover Cleveland, writing verses while Fanny dictated. Displeased, the superintendent told them not to waste the school's time. Believing they were not wasting time, they continued their project. Years later, when Grover Cleveland became President of the United States and Fanny was a noted poet, he many times set aside affairs of state to take dictation from his always welcome White House guest.

Fanny Crosby appeared frequently on the lecture platform and on several occasions addressed both houses of Congress. There she met many of the literary, political, military, and ecclesiastical notables of the day.

Her fame escalated when several collections of her poetry appeared in print and some popular verses such as "Rosalie, the Prairie Flower" and "There's Music in the Air" were set to music, selling thousands of copies.

There is scant information about her marriage. We know that she fell in love with a blind music teacher and church organist, who had been one of her pupils. Alexander Van Alstyne and Fanny Crosby were married on March 5, 1858, and made their home in Brooklyn. They had one child, who died in infancy.

In 1864, at age 44, she set aside work on secular songs and began to author hymns. After five years of hymn writing her fame extended around the world. Of her more than 8,000 hymns, her first ones were the best and most liked. Some were translated into other languages, and at least 70 became popular in England as well as America. Her favorite themes seem to have been heaven and Christ's return.

Since her contract from one publisher called for three hymns a week, she was constantly searching for new material and ideas. Some publishers thought she was putting out too much, so they advised that she write under other names. Among her 200 pen names were her married name, initials, and pseudonyms.

She felt that blindness was an advantage rather than a hindrance. Undisturbed by happenings around her, she could more easily write her poetry. There were days, she confessed, when she could not write a hymn to save her soul. On other days she would compose six or seven, some in as little as 15 minutes.

Though her popularity was enormous, some criticized her work. One judge wrote, "It is more to Mrs. Van Alstyne's credit that she has occasionally found a pearl than that she brought to the surface so many oyster shells." John Julian, an authority on hymnology, thinks her hymns are weak and poor, having only the redeeming features of simplicity and earnestness.

There are recorded stories behind several of her hymns. One time she needed five dollars and could not contact her publisher. After praying, she heard a knock on the door. She talked for awhile with the man at the door who then shook her hand before leaving. She felt something in her hand which turned out to be exactly five dollars. Later she wrote, "My first thought was, it is so wonderful the way the Lord leads me." From this experience came the inspiration for "All the Way My Savior Leads Me."

"Many of my hymns," she said, "were written after experiences in New York mission work." One hot night in the summer of 1869 the blind woman called a cab to take her to a mission service. Word got around that the author of "Pass Me Not" was in the audience, and she was led to the platform. As she spoke she felt that a particular boy must be rescued on that night or maybe not at all. During the invitation to accept Christ she prayed with an 18-year-old who had come to the platform.

Thirty-four years later, when she was speaking at a YMCA meeting, she related the story of the boy. A man came to her after the service and said, "I was the boy .... That evening I sought and found peace. I have tried to live a consistent Christian life ever since. If we never meet again on earth, we will up yonder." He kissed her hand and was gone. Not long afterward she wrote "Rescue the Perishing."

"Blessed Assurance" is probably her most popular hymn. One of Fanny Crosby's closest friends was Phoebe Knapp whose husband, Joseph, founded the Metropolitan Insurance Company. Mrs. Knapp was a musician who published more than 500 hymns herself, and on one of her visits to Fanny she brought a melody she had composed. After playing it through she asked Fanny, "What does the tune say?" The blind poet leaned back in her rocking chair, listened to it a few times,

Professor Hatch was a man of deep piety, faith, and sympathies as shown in one of his poems about heaven. He observes there that some seek heaven for rest, some want to work at projects they cannot accomplish while here in their earthly prison, and some prefer "silent ecstasies" to "articulate utterance." The words he used in bringing the poem to a conclusion are these:

*But in God's perfect heaven*
*All aspirations meet,*
*Each separate longing is fulfilled,*
*Each separate soul complete.*

The music for "Breathe on Me, Breath of God" was composed by Robert Jackson in 1888. The tune name, TRENTHAM, is taken from a small village in Staffordshire, England. In 1868 Robert Jackson followed his father as organist of St. Peter's Church, Oldham, England. He served 48 years, so together they cover about a century, an unequaled record in church music.

This hymn is a prayer which should always be sung thoughtfully and quietly as a true prayer in sincere devotion. In the first stanza we see the words "life anew," "love," and "do." The doing is preceded by the loving, and the loving is preceded by the filling. In the second stanza the union of the human will with the divine will is a natural result when breathing the Breath of God. Compare the third stanza with Psalm 34:5, which reads, "Look to [God], and be radiant." In the fourth stanza immortality is assured through union of the individual soul with the "perfect life" of the "Breath of God."

Scripture References: John 20:22, Ezek. 36:27; Matt. 3:11; Rom. 8:9-11; 2 Cor. 3:17-18; Gal. 5:5, 17-18, 22-25; 1 John 4:13

# America The Beautiful

## Katherine Lee Bates (1859-1929)

*O beautiful for spacious skies, for amber waves of grain;*
*for purple mountain majesties above the fruited plain!*
*America! America! God shed his grace on thee,*
*and crown thy good with brotherhood from sea to shin-*
*ing sea.*

*O beautiful for heroes proved in liberating strife,*
*who more than self their country loved, and mercy more*
*than life!*
*America! America! May God thy gold refine,*
*till all success be nobleness, and every gain divine.*

*O beautiful for patriot dream that sees beyond the years*
*thine alabaster cities gleam, undimmed by human tears!*
*America! America! God mend thine every flaw,*
*confirm thy soul in self-control, thy liberty in law.*

Katherine Lee Bates was born at Falmouth, Massachusetts, into a clergy family. After her college course at Wellesley, she taught high school English for awhile before she returned to Wellesley as an instructor in English Literature. In 1891 she became full professor at Wellesley and remained in that position until 1925. She received an honorary degree from Wellesley and a doctor of literature degree from Middlebury and Oberlin colleges.

Miss Bates's first book of poems was published in 1887, only seven years after her graduation from college. Her approximately two dozen books include poetry, lectures, children's stories and travel records. Beside these, she was editor of many editions of various classics in English and American literature.

Katherine Bates was one of a group of Eastern professors invited to teach in the new summer school started by Colorado College. On her trip to Colorado, her first journey west, she had a glimpse of the great far-stretching fields of golden grain. In a journal of the National Education Association she relates how her friend took her to the great World's Fair, whose "White City" (set in beautiful green gardens) made strong appeal to patriotic feelings. She admits that this view was in large degree responsible for at least one stanza of "America, the Beautiful." "It was with this quickened and deepened sense of America" she writes, "that we went on, my New England eyes delighting in the wind-waved gold of the vast wheat fields."

Before Katherine left Colorado she joined a group going up to Pike's Peak. They rode a prairie wagon part way up and mules the rest of the way to the top. When she reached the peak, although tired from jiggling all the way up, she gazed in awe over the wide expanse of mountain ranges and described the experience as "wordless rapture. It was then and there that the opening lines of 'America the Beautiful' sprang into being." That evening in Colorado Springs the hymn was written out. When she finished her poem she put it in a notebook. There it stayed, forgotten for two years until in 1895 she sent it to a Boston publisher who printed it that same year.

After Katherine retired from teaching she became Professor Emerita. She died at her Wellesley home March 28, 1929.

Out of 60 composers who offered to set these words to music, Samuel A. Ward's music was chosen. During his life (1847-1903) he became a very influential musician and businessman in his home town of Newark, New Jersey. His tune, named MATERNA, was composed for another hymn, "O Mother Dear, Jerusalem," but during World War I it was used for Katherine Bates's hymn.

In beautiful language the hymn describes the richness, beauty, and greatness of our country. It unites the Pilgrims of 1620 with the pilgrims of later days who together made "a thoroughfare for freedom across the wilderness." It shows the heroism and self-sacrifice of Civil War days while it voices the "dream that sees beyond the years." The hymn reminds us that America alone cannot make this dream come true, but it is God who can "shed his grace."

Scripture References: 2 Chron. 7:14; Ps. 33:12; Prov. 14:34

# God Will Take Care Of You

## W. Stillman Martin (1862-1935)
## Civilla Martin (1869-1948)

---

*Be not dismayed whate'er betide,*
*God will take care of you;*
*beneath his wings of love abide,*
*God will take care of you.*

*Refrain:*
*God will take care of you, through every day, o'er all*
*    the way;*
*he will take care of you, God will take care of you.*

*Through days of toil when heart doth fail,*
*God will take care of you;*
*when dangers fierce your path assail,*
*God will take care of you.*

*All you may need he will provide,*
*God will take care of you;*
*nothing you ask will be denied,*
*God will take care of you.*

*No matter what may be the test,*
*God will take care of you;*
*lean, weary one, upon his breast,*
*God will take care of you.*

"God Will Take Care of You" was produced in 1904 by the team ministry of Civilla and W. Stillman Martin. She wrote the text and he composed the music.

The Martins were staying a few weeks at the Practical Bible Training School in Lestershire, New York. He had a speaking engagement at a church some distance from the school. Civilla became ill, so she was unable to accompany him. On that lonely, quiet day she found strength and inspiration in writing this hymn. When her husband came home, he discovered the new poem she had written while he was gone. Immediately, he sat down at their small reed organ and composed the tune as we have it today.

Walter Stillman Martin was born and raised in Rowley, Essex County, Massachusetts, in 1862. After graduating from Harvard University, he was ordained to the Baptist ministry. He soon became well known around the country for his Bible Conferences.

Civilla Durfee Martin was born August 21, 1869, in Nova Scotia. As an adult she studied music and taught school before she married. Following their marriage, the Martins traveled and worked together, holding meetings in many states around the country.

In 1916 the Martins joined the Christian Church (Disciples of Christ) while he was a professor of Bible at the Atlantic Christian College in North Carolina. From 1919 until his death December 16, 1935, they remained at their home in Atlanta, Georgia, while he continued his ministries. Civilla Martin died on March 9, 1948, in Atlanta.

These two dedicated Christian leaders made known God's comforting assurance and loving care through this beautiful hymn of spiritual encouragement.

Scripture References: Deut. 31:8; Ps. 55:22; 57:1; 91:11; 121; Isa. 41:10; Luke 12:6-7; Phil. 4:19; 1 Peter 5:7

# Joyful, Joyful We Adore Thee

## Henry VanDyke (1852-1933)

*Joyful, joyful, we adore thee, God of glory, Lord of love;*
*hearts unfold like flowers before thee, opening to the sun*
*above.*
*Melt the clouds of sin and sadness; drive the dark of*
*doubt away.*
*Giver of immortal gladness, fill us with the light of day!*

*All thy works with joy surround thee, earth and heaven*
*reflect thy rays,*
*stars and angels sing around thee, center of unbroken*
*praise.*
*Field and forest, vale and mountain, flowery meadow,*
*flashing sea,*
*chanting bird and flowing fountain, call us to rejoice in*
*thee.*

*Thou art giving and forgiving, ever blessing, ever blest,*
*wellspring of the joy of living, ocean depth of happy rest!*
*Thou our Father, Christ our brother, all who live in love*
*are thine;*
*teach us how to love each other, lift us to the joy divine.*

*Mortals, join the mighty chorus which the morning stars*
*began;*
*love divine is reigning o'er us, binding all within its span.*
*Ever singing, march we onward, victors in the midst of*
*strife;*
*joyful music leads us sunward, in the triumph song of life.*

47

Coming from Germantown, Pennsylvania, Dr. Henry Van-Dyke lived from 1852 to 1933. He became a Presbyterian minister, college professor and diplomat.

After his graduation from Princeton, he served as pastor of a Presbyterian church in New York City for 17 years. He was called back to his alma mater to be professor of English literature. Later he became United States Minister to The Netherlands and Luxembourg. He published works of prose and poetry, the best-known of which is "The Story of The Other Wise Man." His devotional material, which included 25 books, became best sellers.

The text of this hymn was written while VanDyke was a guest speaker at Williams College in Massachusetts. It is reported that one morning he handed the manuscript to the college president, saying, "Here is a hymn for you. Your mountains (Berkshires) were my inspiration." In giving his purpose for writing these verses he hoped they would present "simple expressions of common Christian feelings and desires in this present time, that may be sung together by people who know the thought of the age, and are not afraid that any truth of science will destroy their religion or that any revolution on earth will overthrow the kingdom of heaven." After he had handed the text to the college president he declared, "It must be sung to the music of Beethoven's 'Hymn of Joy.' "

The tune, HYMN OF JOY, comes from the last movement of Ludwig van Beethoven's Ninth Symphony, published in 1826. This final symphony Beethoven wrote was called the "Choral Symphony" and it is thought to be his best one. It took him six years to compose it. The inspiration came from a poem by Friedrich Schiller called "Ode to Joy." The symphony combined both instruments and voices. Since the composer/director was completely deaf by this time, it has always been a mystery that he could write such beautiful, majestic music.

When the symphony was first performed in Vienna, Austria, with the composer conducting, the soloists had to go to Beethoven and turn him around so he could see the audience applauding. The people were standing, and some were in tears when they realized the extent of his handicap. His music fits VanDyke's words well because they are both expressing joy in God's creation. Beethoven once said, "Every tree seems to speak to me of God. How happy am I to wander through the country as I do."

Beethoven never wrote a tune especially for a hymn, but some of his music has been arranged for hymns. Edward Hodges, the arranger of this hymn music, was originally from England but spent most of his life in New York City as composer, organist and organ builder.

The hymn was first published in VanDyke's *Book of Poems* in 1911. It shows a spirit of optimism, courage, and faith in God. Every line in the first stanza expresses praise and joy. It suggests the gentle, warm influence of sunshine on the flowers. We are offered some special titles for the one we worship, "God of glory" and "Lord of love."

In the second stanza Dr. VanDyke has included both earth and heaven in this universal anthem. Not only "stars and angels" in the realms above, but also "field and forest, flashing sea, chanting bird and flowing fountain." The creators of this hymn want us to join all of nature in a glorious song of joy. It makes us think of several scriptures, but especially Psalm 145:10: "All your works shall give thanks to you, O Lord, and all your faithful shall bless you."

Scripture References: 1 Chron. 16:23-33; Ps. 32:11; 98; Hab. 3:18-19; 1 John 1:5-7
St. 1   Isa. 9:2; 60:19; John 12:36, 46; James 1:17
St. 2   Ps. 19:1; 104:24; 145:10; 148
St. 3   Ps. 103:3-5; 1 Cor. 8:6; 1 John 4:13
St. 4   Job 38:7; 1 Cor. 15:57

# God Of Grace
# And God Of Glory

*Harry Emerson Fosdick (1878-1969)*

---

*God of grace and God of glory, on thy people pour thy
power;
crown thine ancient church's story; bring her bud to glorious flower.
Grant us wisdom, grant us courage,
for the facing of this hour, for the facing of this hour.*

*Lo! the hosts of evil round us scorn thy Christ, assail his
ways!
Fears and doubts too long have bound us; free our hearts
to work and praise.
Grant us wisdom, grant us courage,
for the living of these days, for the living of these days.*

*Cure thy children's warring madness, bend our pride to
thy control;
shame our wanton, selfish gladness, rich in things and
poor in soul.
Grant us wisdom, grant us courage,
lest we miss thy kingdom's goal, lest we miss thy kingdom's goal.*

*Save us from weak resignation to the evils we deplore;
let the search for thy salvation be our glory evermore.
Grant us wisdom, grant us courage,
serving thee whom we adore, serving thee whom we
adore.*

Harry Emerson Fosdick was born in Buffalo, New York, May 24, 1878. He received degrees from Colgate University, Union Theological Seminary, and Columbia University. After he was ordained in 1903, he became pastor of the First Baptist Church of Montclair, New Jersey. During World War I he served as a military chaplain. After the war he became pastor of New York City's First Presbyterian Church while teaching homiletics and theology at Union Theological Seminary.

At this time a beautiful new church was being planned through the generosity of John D. Rockefeller, Jr., who was a member of the congregation. It was to overlook the Hudson River. This Riverside Church was to be racially inclusive and interdenominational. Fosdick was vacationing in Maine in the summer of 1930 and thinking about the new building as well as his new ministry there, when the words of this hymn came to his mind. It would be sung at the opening service on October 5, 1930.

One of his favorite hymn tunes was REGENT SQUARE ("Angels from the Realms of Glory"), for which he wrote these words. His new hymn was published and sung with much enthusiasm for the Riverside Church dedication on February 9, 1931.

Today we sing the text with the tune named CWM RHONDDA, meaning "low valley of Rhondda," composed by John Hughes in 1907. Robert McCutchan joined Fosdick's hymn to Hughes's tune for the 1935 *Methodist Hymnal*. Fosdick was very unhappy and called it his hymn's divorce from REGENT SQUARE and remarriage to CWM RHONDDA. He complained, "The Methodists did it! And both here and abroad they are being followed!" This marriage seems to have endured well in spite of the author's feeling.

While at Riverside Fosdick became well known for his writing, preaching, radio broadcasts and 32 books. His autobiography, *The Living of These Days*, was published in 1956. Harry Emerson Fosdick died in 1969, at the age of 91, but his hymn continues to live. The stanzas begin with prayer and petition, each concluding with "grant us wisdom, grant us courage" to be faithful to Christ.

Scripture References: Deut. 31:6; Ps. 84:11-12; 2 Cor. 1:12; 10:4; Eph. 6:10-17; Phil. 4:13; 2 Tim. 1:7; Heb. 4:16; 13:6; James 1:5

# While Shepherds Watched Their Flocks

## *Nahum Tate (1652-1717)*

---

*While shepherds watched their flocks by night, all seated on the ground,*
*the angel of the Lord came down, and glory shone around,*
*and glory shone around.*

*"Fear not!" said he, for mighty dread had seized their troubled mind.*
*"Glad tidings of great joy I bring to all of humankind,*
*to all of humankind.*

*"To you, in David's town, this day is born of David's line*
*a Savior, who is Christ the Lord, and this shall be the sign,*
*and this shall be the sign:*

*"The heavenly babe you there shall find to human view displayed,*
*all meanly wrapped in swathing bands, and in a manger laid,*
*and in a manger laid."*

*Thus spake the seraph and forthwith appeared a shining throng*
*of angels praising God on high, who thus addressed their song,*
*who thus addressed their song:*

*"All glory be to God on high, and to the earth be peace;*
*good will henceforth from heaven to earth begin and never cease,*
*begin and never cease!"*

Born in Dublin in 1652, Nahum Tate was the son of an Irish preacher and poet. He was educated at Trinity College in Dublin. In 1688 he moved to London and wrote for the stage. He produced a play and wrote "improved versions" of Shakespeare's tragedies. Through a friend he found favor at the court of William and Mary. He received the title Poet Laureate of England and became royal historiographer in 1702.

At this time congregations were still singing only Psalms using the Sternhold-Hopkins Psalter with versified (poetic) Psalms. Singing anything except the Psalms was considered sacrilegious. Paraphrasing Psalms was criticized because it was too showy. They said that David speaks so plainly but "Mr. Tate and others have taken away our Lord, and we know not where they have laid him."

With Dr. Nicolas Brady, Nahum Tate published *The New Version of the Psalms of David* in 1696 to take the place of the "Old Version" and in keeping with the more poetic literary tastes of the day. It received the approval of King William III and became popular in the Church of England. In the second supplement of 1700 there were 16 hymns plus the metrical Psalms. One of these hymns was Tate's Christmas carol about the angels and the shepherds, the only one to be remembered through the years. This supplement, bound with the *Book of Common Prayer*, was used well into the Victorian era. Sadly, due to over-drinking and over-spending, Tate died at a debtors' refuge in London.

The tune CHRISTMAS was adapted from a composition by George Frederick Handel, who was born in Halle, Germany, on February 23, 1685. In 1713 he moved to England where he became a naturalized citizen in 1727. We know him for his oratorio *The Messiah*, which he composed in only 24 days. Handel wrote several tunes especially for hymn texts, but the best known of his tunes were taken from his larger works and arranged for hymns.

Sometimes the wording of hymns has been changed. An early edition of this hymn reads:

*While humble shepherds watched their flocks*
*In Bethlehem's plains by night,*
*An angel sent from heaven appeared*
*And filled the plains with light.*

Scripture Reference: Luke 2:8-14

# Love Divine

## Charles Wesley (1707-1788)

---

*Love divine, all loves excelling, joy of heaven, to earth*
*come down;*
*fix in us thy humble dwelling; all thy faithful mercies*
*crown!*
*Jesus, thou art all compassion, pure, unbounded love*
*thou art;*
*visit us with thy salvation; enter every trembling heart.*

*Breathe, O breathe thy loving Spirit into every troubled*
*breast!*
*Let us all in thee inherit; let us find that second rest.*
*Take away our bent to sinning; Alpha and Omega be;*
*end of faith, as its beginning, set our hearts at liberty.*

*Come, Almighty to deliver, let us all thy life receive;*
*suddenly return and never, nevermore thy temples leave.*
*Thee we would be always blessing, serve thee as thy hosts*
*above,*
*pray and praise thee without ceasing, glory in thy per-*
*fect love.*

*Finish, then, thy new creation; pure and spotless let us be.*
*Let us see thy great salvation perfectly restored in thee;*
*changed from glory into glory, till in heaven we take our*
*place,*
*till we cast our crowns before thee, lost in wonder, love,*
*and praise.*

Charles Wesley was born at Epworth, Lincolnshire, England, on December 18, 1707. He was the 18th child in a family of 19 "preacher's kids." His mother, Susanna, who knew Greek, Latin, and French, taught her children along with the neighbor children for six hours every day. Since she was a devout Christian, she taught them Bible and Christian values. Charles spent 13 years at Westminster school where in public he spoke only Latin. He also sang in the Westminster Abbey choir.

After nine years of study at Oxford, where he formed a "Holy Club," he received a degree in 1728 and later (1735) was ordained in the Church of England. The same year he was sent by the church to America with his brother, John, as a missionary to help the church leaders and to draw the Native Americans to Christianity.

As they crossed the Atlantic by ship they experienced a dangerous storm. They also met a group of German Moravians who, with their spiritual depth, missionary concern and enthusiastic hymn singing, influenced their lives. An account of the storm is recorded in Wesley's journal dated January 25, 1736. "In the midst of the Psalm wherewith the service began, the sea broke over, split the main sail in pieces, covered the ship and poured in between the decks .... A terrible screaming began among the English. The Moravians looked up, and without intermission calmly sang on. I asked one of them afterwards, 'Were you not afraid?' He answered, 'Thank God, no!' "

The Wesleys' stay in America lasted only one year during which Charles became secretary to the governor of Georgia. In that year (1737) their first hymn book was published, edited by John, using Psalm texts or paraphrases by Isaac Watts, Samuel Wesley, Sr., and Samuel Wesley, Jr., since Charles was not yet writing hymns.

They sailed back to England where, in London, they visited the Moravian mission on Aldersgate Street. There they both had deep spiritual experiences. Charles's came first, on May 21, 1738. John's heart was "strangely warmed" three days later. The next 15 to 20 years the brothers became well-known traveling preachers. Riding thousands of miles a year on horseback, they preached three or four times a day at open-air meetings in England, Scotland, Ireland and Wales. Their followers desired a more personal type of spiritual experience with Christ, which they were unable to receive in the Church of England.

On a trip to Wales in 1747, when Charles was 40 years old, he met 20-year-old Sarah (Sally) Gwynne, who was a talented, dedicated Christian. Charles and Sally were married in 1749 and later had eight children, with only three surviving to adulthood. For seven years after their marriage Sally accompanied Charles on his journeys. She led singing at the meetings and, with her beautiful voice, she sang special solos. When Charles developed ill health and they were given a furnished home, they moved from Bristol, the first headquarters of their work, to London where they had another center of ministry.

Charles concentrated on writing hymns. John received the credit for founding the Methodist denomination. Both brothers kept their membership in the Church of England throughout their lives. They wanted to reform the church, not break away. They would attend Anglican services on Sunday mornings and have their Methodist meetings other times during the week in homes and borrowed rooms. They were called Methodists by people who were making fun of them for their methodical ways. But the Wesleys called their gatherings "religious societies of the Church of England." At these meetings they sang some German hymns which John had translated and the new ones Charles was writing.

Charles became so absorbed in his hymn writing one day that he fell off his horse. He later commented, "My companions thought I had broken my neck, but my leg only was bruised, my hand sprained and my head stunned, which spoiled my making of hymns — until the next day."

They used music to help them through their many difficulties. In the mid-1700s there was widespread persecution of the Methodists, and England was at war with France. Their meetings were often broken up by mobs and riots. Many of their preachers were taken before the authorities, as were the Wesleys.

In a small town (Devizes) about 20 miles from Bristol, the local Anglican priest was telling the people that Charles Wesley had preached blasphemy at the university. Some of the town leaders went to the house where the Wesleys were staying. They broke windows, ripped off shutters and drove the brothers' horses into the pond. The next day they used a fire engine to spray water into the house and flooded all the rooms, destroying a store on the first floor. But the Wesleys rode out of town singing Charles's hymn, "Thine Arm Hath Safely Brought Us."

In many villages their followers were threatened, hounded by dogs, and stoned, their businesses ruined and their homes robbed. The Wesleys were considered intruders who were preaching a false doctrine. The Anglican Church leaders were envious of their success. But the lower classes of people were drawn to the Wesleys and enthusiastically sang Charles' hymns about assurance that God would take them to "their eternal home." The Christian Church can break through suffering with rousing songs of great faith and joy to see the miracle of love which dispels fear.

Even when Charles was 80 years old, every day he rode a little horse, "gray with age." When he mounted the horse and was inspired with a hymn subject, he would write it out with his pencil in shorthand on a card kept for that purpose. When he came to the old foundry on London's City Road used for a chapel, he left the pony in the front garden, entered the chapel and cried out, "Pen and ink! Pen and ink!" These were supplied and he completed the hymn he had been composing. When done, he would look around at those present, greet them with kindness, ask after their health, give out a short hymn, and thus "put all in mind of eternity."

Charles Wesley lived in London with Sarah until his death on March 29, 1788. Afterward, when friends went through his house, they found a small basement room boarded up. Inside they discovered 14 volumes of manuscript hymns in the handwriting of John, Charles, and Samuel, their father. Four thousand of them were published in the lifetime of the Wesleys and the rest were left in manuscript form.

Two of Charles and Sarah Wesley's children were musicians, but the most musically talented of all the extended family was their grandson, Samuel Sebastian Wesley (1810-1876), who wrote many hymn tunes we sing. The Wesleys had seven rules for singing which are printed in the front of the 1989 Methodist Hymnal. A portion of the last one reads, "Above all sing spiritually. Have an eye to God in every word you sing. Aim at pleasing Him more than yourself, or any other creature. In order to do this attend strictly to the sense of what you sing, and see that your heart is not carried away with the sound, but offered to God continually."

Charles Wesley wrote over 6,500 hymns (some claim as many as 9,000) and gave believers what his brother John called "a distinct and full account of scriptural Christianity." The Methodists were sometimes mocked for their loud singing of Charles's hymns. On a more positive note one observer wrote, "The song of the Methodists is the most beautiful I ever heard." Earlier the people had not sung hymns since there was no hymn singing in the Anglican Church until it was officially approved in 1820.

Isaac Watts said that Charles's poem "Wrestling Jacob" was worth all that he had ever written. Dr. John Julian in his *Dictionary of Hymnology* claims that "taking quantity and quality into consideration, Charles Wesley was the greatest hymn writer of all ages." In Bristol, there stands by the Methodist chapel a bronze statue of this great man with his words, "O let me commend my Savior to you" on the base of the statue.

"O for a Thousand Tongues," which originally had 18 stanzas, was written in 1739 for the first anniversary of his Aldersgate Church experience. The Moravian leader who drew him closer to Christ was Peter Bohler. When Wesley questioned Bohler, he responded, "Had I a thousand tongues, I would praise Him with them all."

"Hark! the Herald Angels Sing" (1739) was first called "Hymn for Christmas Day" and he began "Hark, how all the welkin (meaning vault of heaven, or sky) sings, Glory to the King of Kings." The famous preacher George Whitfield put it in the form we use today. The tune is an arrangement of a composition by Felix Mendelssohn, who once said, "Singers and hearers will like this work, but it will never be suitable for sacred words."

"Christ the Lord is Risen Today" was written in 1739 to be sung for the opening service at "the foundry Meeting House" in London. It is based on 1 Corinthians 15:5-57. The word "Alleluia," used throughout the hymn, comes from the Hebrew, meaning "Praise ye the Lord." On Easter morning the early Christians would greet each other with the words, "Alleluia, the Lord is risen."

"Jesus, Lover of My Soul," written in 1740, is one of the most popular hymns in the world, translated into virtually all languages. People through several generations have found in it deep refreshment of spirit, and many have had these words on their lips as they passed on to a heavenly life. The text stays today as Wesley wrote it except that the word "be" in phrase six was changed to "is."

"Love Divine" is probably his most popular hymn. In the museum next to the chapel in Bristol you will find a copy of the hymn in Charles's handwritten first manuscript. His sister Kezzy had a breakthrough experience in which she realized Christ's death was for her. Her assurance was so profound and visible that Charles was inspired to write this hymn in 1737. Wesley is saying that Divine love goes far beyond all earthly loves, precious and dear as they are. Jesus Christ's love is "all compassion, pure, unbounded love" for us.

Scripture References: John 14:21; Eph. 3:18-19; 1 John 3:1; 4:7-21
St. 1   Ps. 86:15; 106:4; John 14:16-17
St. 2   John 20:22; Gal. 5:1; Heb. 4:3-11
St. 3   Ps. 145:2; 1 Cor. 2:16-17; Rev. 7:15
St. 4   2 Cor. 3:18; 5:17; 2 Peter 3:13-14

# All Hail The Power Of Jesus' Name

## Edward Perronet (1726-1792)

---

*All hail the power of Jesus' name!*
*Let angels prostrate fall,*
*bring forth the royal diadem,*
*and crown him Lord of all.*

*Ye chosen seed of Israel's race,*
*ye ransomed from the fall,*
*hail him who saves you by his grace,*
*and crown him Lord of all.*

*Sinners, whose love can ne'er forget*
*the wormwood and the gall,*
*go spread your trophies at his feet,*
*and crown him Lord of all.*

*Let every kindred, every tribe*
*on this terrestrial ball,*
*to him all majesty ascribe,*
*and crown him Lord of all.*

*Crown him, ye martyrs of your God,*
*who from his altar call,*
*extol the Stem of Jesse's Rod,*
*and crown him Lord of all.*

*O that with yonder sacred throng*
*we at his feet may fall,*
*We'll join the everlasting song,*
*and crown him Lord of all.*

This hymn has been referred to as the "National Anthem of Christendom." When it was first published in 1779, no author was given. It appeared in *The Gospel Magazine*, which was popular among the "dissenters" breaking away from the Church of England. The magazine's editor was Augustus Toplady, who wrote the hymn "Rock of Ages." Six years later "All Hail the Power of Jesus' Name" was seen in a little book with a long title: *Occasional Verses, Moral and Sacred, published for the instruction and amusement of the dandidly serious and religious.* Another book of verses was found which included this hymn along with an acrostic poem. The first letters of each line spelled Edward Perronet, so it was believed that the book and the hymn were of his authorship.

The date of Edward Perronet's birth is uncertain, but most sources agree on the year 1726. The son of an Anglican priest, at 21 years of age he had a life-changing experience and became a close friend of John and Charles Wesley, all traveling preachers. John Wesley's diary mentions some of Perronet's suffering for the cause: "We were in perils of robbers ... We commended ourselves to God, and rode over the heath singing. Edward Perronet was thrown down and rolled in the mud and mire. Stones were hurled and windows broken. He got a deal of abuse thereby, and not a little dirt, both of which he took very patiently."

Perronet seems to have been a bold, spiritual, successful preacher, but he was also impulsive and restless under the control of the Wesleys. After some years with them, Perronet became convinced that they ought to separate from the Anglican Church and start their own organization. Since the Wesleys were against it, he followed his convictions, withdrew from them, and founded an independent church where he served until his death. It was about that time, at age 58, that he wrote this hymn.

The last words Edward Perronet spoke before his death on January 8, 1792, were these: "Glory to God in the height of His divinity! Glory to God in the depth of His humanity! Glory to God in His all-sufficiency! And into His hands I commend my spirit." He was buried in the cloister of the cathedral at Canterbury.

Perronet's hymn is a song of triumph in times of trouble and persecution. For example, E. P. Scott, a missionary in India, had once ventured into a place where there were murderous natives who had not heard of Christ. He was suddenly confronted by a tribe who pointed their spears at him. Thinking death was near, Scott, who had taken a violin with him, took it out of the case, closed his eyes and began to play, "Let every kindred, every tribe." As he opened his eyes he was relieved to discover a change in the attitudes of his captors. After they invited him to join them, he began two and a half years of successful work among them.

There are three tunes we use with the text. The one called MILES LANE is an English tune. Another one is DIADEM, and the most familiar one is named CORONATION.

The earliest American hymn tune in common use today, CORONATION, was composed by Oliver Holden who lived from 1765 to 1844. He was a native of Massachusetts and lived most of his life in Charlestown, across the river from Boston. He was a carpenter active in rebuilding his home city after its burning by the British in the Revolutionary War. He became a prosperous real estate dealer, was elected to his state legislature, and was a leader in his church.

Holden was the director of many singing schools, wrote music, and compiled hymn books. In one church he built, called the Puritan Church, he served also as its preacher. He was so respected that when George Washington visited Boston in 1789, the city authorized Holden to write the music and words as well as train the male choir that would sing this triumphal hymn as Washington reached the Old State House, which now houses the little four and a half octave organ he played. His lament before he died was, "I have some beautiful airs running through my head, if I only had strength to note them down." Oliver Holden died at the age of 77 on September 4, 1844.

64

You may guess that the reason for calling this tune CORO-NATION is that it fits so well with the words of the hymn about crowning Jesus Christ as the highest of all royalty.

Scripture References: Zech. 14:9; Phil. 2:9-11; Col. 1:15-19; Rev. 5:13, 11:15
St. 1 Ps. 148:2; Rev. 5:11-13; 7:11-12
St. 2 Deut. 7:6-9; Eph. 1:4-6; 1 Peter 2:9; Rev. 17:14
St. 4 Ps. 145:21

# Angels From The Realms Of Glory

## James Montgomery (1771-1854)

*Angels from the realms of glory,*
*wing your flight o'er all the earth;*
*ye who sang creation's story*
*now proclaim Messiah's birth:*

*Refrain:*
*Come and worship, come and worship,*
*worship Christ, the newborn King.*

*Shepherds, in the field abiding,*
*watching o'er your flocks by night,*
*God with us is now residing;*
*yonder shines the infant light:*

*Sages, leave your contemplations,*
*brighter visions beam afar;*
*seek the great Desire of nations;*
*ye have seen his natal star:*

*Saints, before the altar bending,*
*watching long in hope and fear;*
*suddenly the Lord, descending,*
*in his temple shall appear:*

The parents of James Montgomery, who authored "Angels From the Realms of Glory," died when they were Moravian missionaries in the West Indies and James was only six years old. A Brethren school (Moravian Seminary) in Fulneck, England, took over the care of this young boy and instilled in him Christian ideals.

When he was ten years old he began to write serious poetry. When he was 16 he left his hometown and worked as a store clerk in two different towns. He also went from place to place trying to sell his poetry, but no one seemed interested. For a while he worked in a grocery store. Finally he became assistant and then editor of a newspaper in Sheffield, England. He kept that job for 31 years.

Twice he was put in prison for his outspoken stand against the Tory government, in control at that time. Many of his hymns were written in prison. He strongly supported foreign missions, Bible societies, and the abolition of slavery. He was always ready to assist the poor and downtrodden.

At age 43 he went back to his parents' Moravian church. His words are: "On my birthday, after many delays and misgivings and repentings, I wrote to Fulneck for readmission into the Brethren congregation; and on Sunday last I was publicly invested with my title to that goodly heritage."

In 1825 he gave up his newspaper to devote himself to writing and promoting missions. In 1833 he was widely recognized and awarded an annual pension of 1,000 pounds by the government as a reward for his many contributions to English society.

He wrote about 400 hymns although this is considered his greatest and, by some, the best of the Advent hymns. This hymn was published in *The Iris* (his newspaper) on Christmas eve, 1816. It was first titled "Good Tidings of Great Joy to All People."

During his last illness, his doctor read aloud to him many of his hymns to give him comfort. On April 29, 1854, the Reverend Montgomery led an evening meeting. The next morning some friends found him lying unconscious on the floor of his home, and he never awakened. John Julian, an authority on hymnology, has written: "Montgomery's devotional spirit was of the noblest type. With the faith of a strong man he united the beauty and simplicity of a child. Richly poetic without exuberance, dogmatic without uncharitableness, tender without sentimentality, elaborate without diffusiveness, richly musical without apparent effort, he has bequeathed to the church wealth which could only come from true genius and a sanctified heart.''

The tune name is REGENT SQUARE, named after Regent Square Presbyterian Church in London. Henry Smart (1813-1879), the composer, was the nephew of Sir George Smart, organist of St. George's Windsor, and the son of a violinist. After a position as lawyer for four years, he changed to that of musician. Even though he had little formal training, he was one of the best organists and composers in the British Isles. He was totally blind the last 15 years of his life, but continued to play and write. His daughter wrote down the music as he played it for her. He also designed and built some of England's finest organs. He died in 1879 at age 66.

The theme of the hymn is ''come and worship Christ, the newborn King.'' The first stanza invites the angels ''to proclaim Messiah's birth.'' In stanza two the invitation is extended to the shepherds and in stanza three, to the wise men. The word ''saints'' in stanza four refers to Simeon and Anna, who saw the child Jesus in the temple.

Scripture References:
St. 1   Luke 2:10-14; Heb. 1:6
St. 2   Matt. 1:23; Luke 2:8-20; John 1:9
St. 3   Matt. 2:1-12
St. 4   Mal. 3:1

# What A Friend We Have In Jesus

## *Joseph Scriven (1819-1886)*

---

*What a friend we have in Jesus,*
*all our sins and griefs to bear!*
*What a privilege to carry*
*everything to God in prayer!*
*O what peace we often forfeit,*
*O what needless pain we bear,*
*all because we do not carry*
*everything to God in prayer.*

*Have we trials and temptations?*
*Is there trouble anywhere?*
*We should never be discouraged;*
*take it to the Lord in prayer.*
*Can we find a friend so faithful*
*who will all our sorrows share?*
*Jesus knows our every weakness;*
*take it to the Lord in prayer.*

*Are we weak and heavy laden,*
*cumbered with a load of care?*
*Precious Savior, still our refuge;*
*take it to the Lord in prayer.*
*Do thy friends despise, forsake thee?*
*Take it to the Lord in prayer!*
*In his arms he'll take and shield thee;*
*thou wilt find a solace there.*

This popular hymn is usually the first one missionaries teach their people. But the story behind it is sad.

Joseph Scriven was born in Dublin, Ireland, of prosperous parents in 1819. He graduated from Trinity College, fell in love and was soon to be married. The day before the wedding his fiancee's dead body was pulled from a pool of water where she had accidentally drowned. Scriven was overcome with shock and grief.

He tried to forget by moving a great distance away. The Plymouth Brethren who drew him away from his parents and toward Canada were an influence in his life. He tried to forget, but could not. He was a person of high ideals with a melancholic personality. He settled in a small Canadian town and for 40 years he associated himself with the poor, the sick, and the widows. He tutored some as he also worked at simple labor such as sawing wood and carpentry.

For many years it was thought that the hymn was written by another author, Horatius Bonar. Discovering his name on it, Mr. Bonar disclaimed any connection with it, so it was marked "Author Unknown."

Years later a friend visiting Scriven during an illness found the words on his bedside table and asked if he had written them. The modest Irishman replied, "The Lord and I wrote it between us." Scriven explained that he had written the hymn to send to his sick mother in Dublin for her comfort.

On October 10, 1886, Joseph Scriven was found dead. His body, like his sweetheart's years before, was pulled from a pool of water. Grief fell over the community. Some believed his death was accidental. But the poor, those who knew him best, wondered if Scriven had taken his own life. His friends erected a monument in his memory which read: "Four miles north of Pengally's cemetery lies the philanthropist and author of this great masterpiece written at Port Hope, 1857." With the inscription were the stanzas of Scriven's hymn. In 1869 a small collection of his poems and hymns was published titled *Hymns and Other Verses*.

The tune, now called CONVERSE, was first named ERIE, probably from Erie, Pennsylvania, where the composer, Charles G. Converse (1834-1918) lived. He received his musical education in Germany, where he was acquainted with the famous composer Franz Liszt. Returning to America, he studied law and had his practice for many years in Erie. He wrote literature as well as music and was an inventor and an organ manufacturer. Although he composed cantatas, oratorios, and chorales, this hymn tune is his only music to become well-known.

Carlton R. Young writes, "This hymn in its warm, musical setting extends the intimate characterization of Jesus as a mother, gently rocking and comforting a child, to a friend who shares and bears our sorrows, hears our prayers, and carries them to God."

Scripture References: Ps. 6:9; 55:22; 57:1; John 15:13-16; Phil. 4:6; 1 Thess. 5:17; 1 Peter 5:7; 1 John 5:14-15

# Stand Up, Stand Up For Jesus

## George Duffield (1818-1888)

---

*Stand up, stand up for Jesus, ye soldiers of the cross;*
*lift high his royal banner, it must not suffer loss.*
*From victory unto victory his army shall he lead,*
*till every foe is vanquished, and Christ is Lord indeed.*

*Stand up, stand up for Jesus, the trumpet call obey;*
*forth to the mighty conflict, in this his glorious day.*
*Ye that are brave now serve him against unnumbered*
*    foes;*
*let courage rise with danger, and strength to strength*
*    oppose.*

*Stand up, stand up for Jesus, stand in his strength alone;*
*the arm of flesh will fail you, ye dare not trust your own.*
*Put on the gospel armor, each piece put on with prayer;*
*where duty calls or danger, be never wanting there.*

*Stand up, stand up for Jesus, the strife will not be long;*
*this day the noise of battle, the next the victor's song.*
*To those who vanquish evil a crown of life shall be;*
*they with the King of Glory shall reign eternally.*

George Duffield was born in Carlisle, Pennsylvania, September 12, 1818, into an active Presbyterian family. He studied at Yale University and Union Theological Seminary. After a pastorate of four years in New Jersey, he accepted a call from a church in Philadelphia, where he wrote this hymn. His situation was difficult as he found a mortgaged church building, people relocating and a diminishing congregation who were unable to meet their financial obligations. He had some results on the spiritual side, but with all the threatening conditions in the church, he became discouraged. Each year the congregation decreased in numbers.

At about this time (1858) a revival was going on in Philadelphia. In connection with it were the noon prayer meetings in charge of the Young Men's Christian Association, whose leader was a young Episcopalian clergyman, Dudley Tyng. Although he was not yet 30 years old, he was well known for his fervor, Christian zeal, and strong preaching against slavery.

Due to the controversy over slavery, Tyng had to retire from his church. Soon he started the Church of the Covenant, whose congregation quickly grew. During his sermon at a prayer meeting for about 5,000 men he remarked, "I must tell my Master's errand, and I would rather that this right arm were amputated at the trunk than that I should come short of my duty to you in delivering God's message." Some of the clergy in the city were supporting Tyng in his views as was the Reverend Duffield.

A week after the sermon on April 13, 1858, Mr. Tyng went from the study of his country home to the barn floor where a mule was at work treading a machine for shelling corn. As he patted the animal on the neck his sleeve became caught in the cogs of the wheel and his arm was torn up. After an amputation, he died. Just before he died he was asked to give any messages he might have for those devoted to him and his work. He began his short message with the words, "Tell them, 'Let us all stand up for Jesus.' "

These words were quoted by ministers at various services including the Reverend Tyng's funeral, where the Reverend Duffield was present. On the Sunday following the funeral Duffield read these verses he had written for the conclusion of his sermon. The Sunday School Superintendent had them printed on a fly leaf, they were copied by religious papers, and they appeared in *The Sabbath Hymn Book* (Congregational) that same year and in *The Church Psalmist* (Presbyterian) in the next year. It is now sung all around the world. According to Duffield's son, "a cob of corn from that threshing-floor has hung ever since on the study wall of the author."

George Duffield continued on with his declining church until 1861 when he resigned his pastorate. He went on to pastor other places in several states for 40 years of active service. His last years he lived in Bloomfield, New Jersey, with his son, who also was a poet. The son preceded his father in death by a year.

Some hymnals have two different tunes for this hymn. One is by Adam Geibel (1885-1933), who lived in Philadelphia. His blindness did not stop him from his work as organist, conductor and composer. The more familiar tune comes from a secular piece by George Webb (1803-1887), who made his home in Boston. Hymnologist Louis Benson observes, "This is an instance of a hymn making its way without the aid of a tune."

God uses many people in many circumstances to bring our hymns to birth. Kenneth Osbeck in his book *101 Hymn Stories* sums it up well. "A dynamic young Episcopalian preacher, a corn-threshing machine, a tragic fatal accident, a Presbyterian minister's hymn text tribute, two tunes — one secular and another by a blind composer — and the revival of 1858, the work of God in Philadelphia, still have their influence on us today each time we open our hymnals to this hymn."

Scripture References: Rom. 8:37; 1 Cor. 15:55-58; 16:13; Eph. 6:10-20; Phil. 1:27-30; 1 Tim. 6:12; 2 Tim. 2:3-4; 4:7-8; Heb. 10:23

# I Love To Tell The Story

## *Katherine Hankey (1834-1911)*

---

*I love to tell the story of unseen things above,*
*of Jesus and his glory, of Jesus and his love.*
*I love to tell the story, because I know 'tis true;*
*it satisfies my longings as nothing else can do.*

*Refrain:*
*I love to tell the story, 'twill be my theme in glory,*
*to tell the old, old story of Jesus and his love.*

*I love to tell the story; more wonderful it seems*
*than all the golden fancies of all our golden dreams.*
*I love to tell the story, it did so much for me;*
*and that is just the reason I tell it now to thee.*

*I love to tell the story; 'tis pleasant to repeat*
*what seems, each time I tell it, more wonderfully sweet.*
*I love to tell the story, for some have never heard*
*the message of salvation from God's own holy Word.*

*I love to tell the story, for those who know it best*
*seem hungering and thirsting to hear it like the rest.*
*And when, in scenes of glory, I sing the new, new song,*
*'twill be the old, old story that I have loved so long.*

Katherine Hankey came from a wealthy banking family in Clapham, England, an elite suburb of London. Her father was a member of a group of influential Christian laymen called the Clapham Sect. Early in her life Kate, as she was affectionately called, organized Sunday School classes for the poor as well as the rich in her Anglican church.

One particular Sunday School class was for girls who worked in the London shops. Another class was for the girls of a higher social circle. These classes were influential throughout the city in guiding young students to become strong Christian workers.

Along with her teaching she wrote a book on confirmation called *Bible Class Teachings* and several books of poetry. Her money from these books was given to foreign missions after she had made a trip to South Africa to care for her invalid brother.

At the early age of 30 Katherine became very ill. While she was recovering, she wrote a long poem in two parts about the life of Christ. It contained 50 verses. The first section was titled "The Story Wanted," which later was adapted for the hymn "Tell Me the Old, Old Story." That same year (1868) she completed the second part, which was called "The Story Told." From that second section came the hymn "I Love to Tell the Story." Kate also had musical ability, so she wrote tunes for her texts. But the hymns did not receive much notice with her music. Other tunes were composed for her hymns.

At a large gathering in Montreal, Canada, a preacher quoted Katherine's poems at the close of his sermon. In the audience was William H. Doane, composer of an extensive number of hymn tunes. Mr. Doane was so moved that he composed musical settings for her texts. Later a new tune replaced Doane's music. The music we now use (HANKEY) was composed by William G. Fischer (1835-1912), a Philadelphia college music teacher and piano dealer who also added the refrain.

Along with the illness, suffering and early death of Katherine Hankey this hymn of love to Jesus Christ was born that we might be inspired as we sing.

Scripture References: Ps. 66:16; Isa. 63:7; John 3:16-17; Acts 1:8; 1 Peter 3:15; 1 John 4:14

# O Little Town Of Bethlehem

## Phillips Brooks (1835-1893)

*O little town of Bethlehem, how still we see thee lie;*
*above thy deep and dreamless sleep the silent stars go by.*
*Yet in thy dark streets shineth the everlasting light;*
*the hopes and fears of all the years are met in thee tonight.*

*For Christ is born of Mary, and gathered all above,*
*while mortals sleep, the angels keep their watch of won-*
*   dering love.*
*O morning stars together, proclaim the holy birth,*
*and praises sing to God the King, and peace to all on*
*   earth!*

*How silently, how silently, the wondrous gift is given;*
*so God imparts to human hearts the blessings of his*
*   heaven.*
*No ear may hear his coming, but in this world of sin,*
*where meek souls will receive him, still the dear Christ*
*   enters in.*

*O holy Child of Bethlehem, descend to us, we pray;*
*cast out our sin, and enter in, be born in us today.*
*We hear the Christmas angels the great glad tidings tell;*
*O come to us, abide with us, our Lord Emmanuel!*

Phillips Brooks, born December 13, 1835, was influenced
to appreciate hymns when he was a child. Family devotions
were important to his parents. On Sundays each child, when
old enough, would recite a hymn from memory. By the time
Brooks went to college he could quote about 200 hymns.

After graduation from Harvard and the Episcopal Theological Seminary in Virginia (1859), he ministered in Episcopal churches of Philadelphia and Boston. He also taught at the Philadelphia Divinity School. At the church he was asked to write special music for the Sunday School Christmas celebration in 1868.

As he was considering the assignment, he thought back on an experience he had two years earlier in the country of Jesus' birth and life. He had ridden a horse from Jerusalem to Bethlehem on Christmas eve and stopped on a hill where he looked out over Bethlehem. In his imagination he saw again the events of the first Christmas. With these thoughts in mind, Brooks attended a midnight service and prayed, "O Holy Child of Bethlehem, descend to us, we pray; cast out our sin, and enter in; be born in us today." So his prayer was in verse form as he continued to pray.

After writing the words he took the poem to his organist/Sunday School superintendent, Louis Redner (1831-1908), saying, "If you will write a suitable tune for these words, I will name it for you." But on Christmas eve the tune had still not come to the organist who admitted, "I thought more about my Sunday School lesson than I did about the music." Discouraged concerning the music, he went to bed. During the night he said he heard an angel-strain whispering in his ear. Waking, he took his pen and jotted down a melody. On Sunday morning before church he filled in the harmony. Neither man expected the carol or the music would live beyond that Christmas. There have been other tunes composed for the text, but Mr. Redner's ST. LOUIS has lasted in popularity.

Phillips Brooks was one of the most respected preachers of the nineteenth century. He is only known today for this hymn and his classic *Lectures on Preaching*. His personality and deep insight into common human experiences drew such crowds that they pushed out the regular parishioners from his worship services. He drew high praise from Christian people of every denomination. Even though he never married, most of the few hymns he wrote were for children as he loved children and liked to romp with them on the nursery floor.

Phillips Brooks was appointed Bishop over all the Episcopal churches in Massachusetts in 1891. He died unexpectedly on January 23, 1893, and was mourned by all who knew him. A story which circulated after his death is about a five-year-old girl who wondered why she hadn't seen her preacher for several days. When her mother explained that Bishop Brooks had gone to heaven, the child exclaimed, "Oh, Mama, how happy the angels will be."

Beside Trinity Church in Boston there is a statue of Phillips Brooks with the figure of Christ standing behind him, always his inspiration. Even though we may not see the statue we will always remember his beautiful carol sung each Christmas.

The last verse of another of his Christmas hymns reads:

*Then let every heart keep its Christmas within,*
*Christ's pity for sorrow, Christ's hatred for sin,*
*Christ's care for the weakest, Christ's courage for right,*
*Christ's dread of the darkness, Christ's love of the light;*
*Everywhere, everywhere, Christmas tonight.*

Scripture References: Matt. 1:18-23; 2:1-2; Luke 2:1-7, 11; Micah 5:2

# Beneath The Cross Of Jesus

## Elizabeth Clephane (1830-1869)

---

*Beneath the cross of Jesus I fain would take my stand,*
*the shadow of a mighty rock within a weary land;*
*a home within the wilderness, a rest upon the way,*
*from the burning of the noontide heat, and the burden*
*of the day.*

*Upon that cross of Jesus mine eye at times can see*
*the very dying form of One who suffered there for me;*
*and from my stricken heart with tears two wonders I*
*confess:*
*the wonders of redeeming love and my unworthiness.*

*I take, O cross, thy shadow for my abiding place;*
*I ask no other sunshine than the sunshine of his face;*
*content to let the world go by, to know no gain nor loss,*
*my sinful self my only shame, my glory all the cross.*

Elizabeth Clephane lived only 39 years. She was the third daughter of a sheriff living in Edinburgh. As a little girl she became an orphan. She was small of stature, quiet, shy, and bookish, as she was the head of her school classes.

She was sensitive to the needs and sorrows of those around her. When she later moved to Melrose, Scotland, she became known among the poor and suffering of the community as "the sunbeam," due to her cheery, helpful nature. She spent all of her income, beyond her necessities, on helping others.

Eight of her hymns were published in a periodical for Christian homes called *The Family Treasury*. She is remembered for two well-known hymns. In 1868 she wrote "The Ninety and Nine" for a friend who used it as a contribution to *The Children's Hour* magazine.

Five years after her death the famous preacher, Dwight L. Moody, and Ira D. Sankey, his musician, were on a train together in Scotland, where they were holding special meetings. Their church had been destroyed three years earlier in the great Chicago fire. As they were traveling, Moody was working through some unopened letters from home to find out how the new tabernacle was progressing. Sankey, at the same time, was scanning a newspaper and happened to notice a poem called "The Ninety and Nine" written by Elizabeth Clephane. After he read the lines over several times, he tore the poem out of the newspaper and put it in his pocket.

Later at the Edinburgh meetings it came time for Sankey to sing his solo. He had not expected the sermon subject of the evening, which was "The Good Shepherd"; therefore, he had no appropriate number. He thought of the poem in his pocket, put it on the piano rack, his hands hit the keys and he started to play as he sang the text. This may be the only case in the history of hymnmaking where a tune stayed just as the composer sang it the first time. (Elizabeth Clephane's two sisters were in that service.)

"Beneath the Cross of Jesus" appeared in 1868, a year before Miss Clephane's death. The hymn was probably written in the midst of pain and suffering, but it shows how faith can lead from suffering to song.

All of Elizabeth Clephane's hymns were published by William Arnot under the title *Breathing On the Border*. An introduction in the book explains that it was "written on the very edge of this life with the better land fully in view."

Scripture References: Isa. 32:2; Luke 9:23; 1 Cor. 1:17-18; Gal. 6:14

# I Need Thee Every Hour

## Annie Sherwood Hawks (1835-1918)

---

*I need thee every hour, most gracious Lord;*
*no tender voice like thine can peace afford.*

*Refrain:*
*I need thee, O I need thee; every hour I need thee;*
*O bless me now, my Savior, I come to thee.*

*I need thee every hour; stay thou nearby;*
*temptations lose their power when thou art nigh.*

*I need thee every hour, in joy or pain;*
*come quickly and abide, or life is vain.*

*I need thee every hour; teach me thy will;*
*and thy rich promises in me fulfill.*

*I need thee every hour, most Holy One;*
*O make me thine indeed, thou blessed Son.*

The writer of this prayer hymn was Annie Sherwood Hawks, who was born May 28, 1835, at Hoosick, New York. She contributed poems to newspapers when she was only 14 years old. After her marriage to Charles Hawks and while raising three children, she lived in Brooklyn, where she was a member of the Hanson Place Baptist Church. Her pastor, Dr. Robert Lowry, encouraged her to keep writing, since he was also a hymnist. This is the only one of her 400 hymns that has lasted.

An experience of the presence of God with her caused the birth of this hymn in 1872. Mrs. Hawks was not in a church worship service at the time but in her own home busy with the tasks of ordinary housework. She explained that the rooms around seemed to be like the house of God and the gate of heaven. Years later she wrote these words: "I was so filled with a sense of nearness to my Master that wondering how one could live without him in either joy or pain, these words, 'I need thee every hour' were flashed into my mind." She goes on to describe the place and time. "Seating myself by the open window in the balmy air of the bright June day, I caught up my pencil and the words were soon committed to paper, almost as they are being sung now."

Sometime after this inspirational writing, Annie experienced deep suffering which may have been caused by the death of her husband in 1888. Later she wrote, "It was not until years after, when the shadow fell over my way, the shadow of a great loss, that I understood something of the comforting power in the words which I had been permitted to give out to others in my hours of sweet security and peace." After her husband's death, she lived with her daughter in Bennington, Vermont, until she died at age 82.

The verses were given to her pastor, the Reverend Lowry, who composed the tune and added the refrain. Their hymn was first published in a little pamphlet of hymns for the National Baptist Sunday School Convention held in Cincinnati, Ohio, in 1872. The hymn soon found its way first into Sunday School hymnbooks and on into present day church hymnals. Now, singing it helps many Christians through times of discouragement, sorrow and suffering.

Scripture References: Ps. 40:17; 73:28; 86:1-10; Isa. 55:6; Acts 17:27-28; Heb. 4:16
St. 1    Isa. 26:3; John 16:33
St. 2    1 Cor. 10:13; Heb. 2:18

# It Is Well With My Soul

## Horatio G. Spafford (1828-1888)

*When peace, like a river, attendeth my way,*
*when sorrows like sea billows roll;*
*whatever my lot, thou hast taught me to say,*
*It is well, it is well with my soul.*

*Refrain:*
*It is well with my soul, it is well, it is well with my soul.*

*Though Satan should buffet, though trials should come,*
*let this blest assurance control,*
*that Christ has regarded my helpless estate,*
*and hath shed his own blood for my soul.*

*My sin, oh, the bliss of this glorious thought!*
*My sin, not in part but the whole,*
*is nailed to the cross, and I bear it no more,*
*praise the Lord, praise the Lord, O my soul!*

*And, Lord, haste the day when my faith shall be sight,*
*the clouds be rolled back as a scroll;*
*the trump shall resound, and the Lord shall descend,*
*even so, it is well with my soul.*

The successful Chicago lawyer and Presbyterian layman, Horatio G. Spafford, was born in North Troy, New York, on October 20, 1828. In his forties this teacher of medical law suffered two great tragedies. The first one, although very discouraging, did not compare to the second in seriousness. He had purchased a large amount of real estate on the shore of

Lake Michigan but in 1871, due to the great Chicago fire, his holdings were completely destroyed.

Shortly before the fire he had experienced the death of his son. Hoping for a rest, along with helping the popular Christian speaker Dwight L. Moody in his Great Britain meetings, Spafford decided to sail to Europe with his wife and four daughters. Due to some unexpected business he had to remain in Chicago. It was decided that the rest of the family would sail as planned. On November 22, 1873, in mid-ocean their large ship, the *S. S. Ville du Havre*, was struck by the English ship, *Lochearn*, and soon sank. During those last few minutes Mrs. Spafford collected her four little girls, knelt with them and asked God to spare their lives, if possible, or to make them ready to die. The children had accepted Christ in Chicago. Within half an hour their ship had sunk and the Spafford girls along with about 220 other passengers drowned.

Mrs. Spafford, after being tossed around in the waves awhile, was rescued by a sailor rowing a small boat over the place where the ship sank. He took her to Cardiff, Wales, where she sent word back to her husband in Chicago. The two words on the cablegram were "Saved alone." When he read it, he remarked to a friend, "I am glad to trust Christ when it costs me something." On the way across the Atlantic to meet his wife, the captain showed Mr. Spafford where the tragedy happened. As he stood on the deck looking at the waves, he wrote the hymn that was to give comfort to many people.

Back in Chicago the Spaffords had two more children. In 1881 Mr. and Mrs. Spafford and their daughter Bertha moved to Jerusalem, where they lived for the remainder of their lives. After his death in 1888, Bertha continued their ministry to the unfortunate of that country, especially children. Married, Bertha Spafford Vester ran the American Colony Hotel as well as a hospital for children. She painted wild flowers of the area to sell and raise money for her work. In 1962 the newscaster Lowell Thomas wrote about her life and work.

The story of the tune composer also involves a tragedy. Philip Bliss, born July 9, 1838, in Clearfield County, Pennsylvania, later became music director at First Congregational

Church of Chicago and published two books titled *The Charm* (1871) and *Sunshine* (1873). When he became involved with the preaching campaigns of D. L. Moody and his musician Ira D. Sankey, Bliss gave up his music publishing company. Spafford's text impressed him so much that he wrote a tune (VILLE DU HAVRE) which was published with the hymn in 1876. He was a prolific writer of hymns, texts as well as tunes.

This hymn was the last Philip Bliss ever sang. It was the closing hymn at a meeting in Peoria, Illinois. From there he and his wife traveled to Rome, Pennsylvania, to visit their two sons for the Christmas holidays. December 29, 1876, on the way back to Chicago for more services, their train approached Ashtabula, Ohio, where a bridge collapsed, plunging the train and seven cars into the icy water below. Many people were drowned and many others were trapped in the wreckage or died in the fire caused by the wreck. Mr. Bliss could have escaped but did not want to leave his wife. Eighty to ninety people lost their lives, which made it the worst train wreck up to that time. Friends who searched for days could never find their bodies. Some of his popular hymns are "Hallelujah, What a Savior," "Wonderful Words of Life," and "Jesus Loves Even Me."

This hymn was born out of suffering. A friend of Horatio Spafford who was hurting read these words and remarked, "If Spafford could feel like that after suffering all he suffered, I will cease my complaints and will bravely bear my affliction."

Scripture References: Ps. 103:1-4; Rom. 8:28; 15:13; 2 Cor. 5:7; Gal. 2:20; 2 Tim. 1:12; Heb. 10:22
St. 2   Eph. 6:16; Heb. 2:14; 1 John 3:8
St. 3   1 Cor. 15:3; 2 Cor. 5:21
St. 4   Matt. 24:30-31; 1 Cor. 15:53

# My Faith Looks Up To Thee

## Ray Palmer (1808-1887)

*My faith looks up to thee,*
*thou Lamb of Calvary, Savior divine!*
*Now hear me while I pray,*
*take all my guilt away,*
*O let me from this day be wholly thine!*

*May thy rich grace impart*
*strength to my fainting heart, my zeal inspire!*
*As thou hast died for me,*
*O may my love to thee*
*pure, warm, and changeless be, a living fire!*

*While life's dark maze I tread,*
*and griefs around me spread, be thou my guide;*
*bid darkness turn to day,*
*wipe sorrow's tears away,*
*nor let me ever stray from thee aside.*

*When ends life's transient dream,*
*when death's cold, sullen stream shall o'er me roll;*
*blest Savior, then in love,*
*fear and distrust remove;*
*O bear me safe above, a ransomed soul!*

Ray Palmer, the son of a judge, was born on November 12, 1808, in Little Compton, Rhode Island. After he was forced to quit school at age 13, he found work as a store clerk in Boston. Under the influence of his pastor at Park Street

Congregational Church, he decided to follow Christ, and soon he felt God's call to become a minister. Because his pastor encouraged him to continue his education, he attended Andover Academy where he was a classmate of the famous writer, Oliver Wendell Holmes.

In 1830 Ray was 22 and had just graduated from Yale University. He was lonely, discouraged, in ill health, had no money and was burdened with a feeling of religious uncertainty. While translating two verses of a German poem about coming to the cross, he had a vision of faith. It was, he said, "an hour when Christ in the riches of his grace and love was so vividly apprehended as to fill the soul with deep emotion."

The hymn was written and copied into the little notebook which he kept in his pocket. He says, "The stanzas came with little effort ... I composed them with a deep consciousness of my own needs, without the slightest thought of writing for another eye and least of all of writing a hymn for Christian worship." Soon after this experience he found a job teaching for a girls' school in New York. Following 1835, when he was ordained as a Congregational minister, he served two long pastorates in Maine and New York.

Lowell Mason (1792-1872), the composer of the tune OLIVET, was the founder of public school music teaching and received the first doctor's degree in music given in the United States. Lowell Mason and Ray Palmer met one day in front of a store in Boston. Mason was a busy man directing three choirs, trying to get a new music course started in the public schools and compiling material for his book *Spiritual Songs for Social Worship*. He was glad to make contact with Palmer since he wanted him to write some verses for his new book. Palmer found his pocket notebook and showed Mason the verses he had written two years earlier. The composer hurried into a nearby store, borrowed a piece of paper and copied the poem. Handing the notebook back to Palmer, Mason said, "Mr. Palmer, you may live many years and do many good things but posterity will remember you as the author of 'My Faith Looks Up to Thee.' "

That night in his study Lowell Mason set to music Ray Palmer's first and greatest hymn. Mason was right. Ray Palmer has gone down in history for writing that one poem. So also has Lowell Mason's music played a large part in this hymn as well as nearly 700 others.

Ray Palmer accomplished much during his lifetime. Other than his two churches he was secretary of the American Congregational Missions Program. He authored several volumes of poems and devotional essays along with his 37 hymns for which he would never accept payment. In 1878 he developed ill health and moved to Newark, New Jersey, where he continued to write and act as supply pastor until his death in 1887.

Once again two talented people have blended their work together to form a beautiful, meaningful response for us to offer God in worship. It has been thought that the first stanza of the hymn is a prayer of consecration. The second stanza is a prayer for perseverance, zeal and love. The third and fourth stanzas are prayer for sustaining grace and divine guidance.

Scripture References: Jer. 33:8; Rom. 1:16-17; 5:1-2; Eph. 3:12; Heb. 12:2
St. 1    John 1:29
St. 2    2 Cor. 4:16; 12:9; Titus 2:14
St. 3    Ps. 73:24; Isa. 60:20

# Thou Didst Leave Thy Throne

## Emily Elliott (1836-1897)

---

*Thou didst leave thy throne and thy kingly crown*
*When thou camest to earth for me;*
*But in Bethlehem's home there was found no room*
*For thy holy nativity:*

*Refrain:*
*O come to my heart, Lord Jesus!*
*There is room in my heart for thee.*

*Heaven's arches rang when the angels sang,*
*Proclaiming thy royal degree;*
*But in lowly birth thou didst come to earth,*
*And in great humility:*

*The foxes found rest and the birds their nest*
*In the shade of the forest tree;*
*But thy couch was the sod, O thou Son of God,*
*In the desert of Galilee:*

*Thou camest, O Lord, with the living Word*
*That should set thy people free;*
*But with mocking scorn, and with crown of thorn,*
*They bore thee to Calvary:*

*When the heavens shall ring, and the angels sing,*
*At thy coming to victory,*
*Let thy voice call me home, saying, "Yet there is room,*
*There is room at my side for thee:"*

Emily Elliott was born in Brighton, England, on July 22, 1836. She came from a hymn-loving and hymn-writing family. Her father and uncle wrote and published one book of hymns which also included 11 hymns written by an aunt. Another of her aunts was Charlotte Elliott who wrote "Just As I Am," which has been used extensively through the years.

For six years Emily edited a magazine called *The Church Missionary Juvenile Instructor.* She published two volumes of hymns and poems in the 1870s. Forty-eight of her hymns were published in a book titled *Under the Pillow.* It was in large type to be used especially for hospitals, nursing homes and ill people in general. Her interest and endeavor included rescue missions and Sunday Schools in her area.

This hymn text was privately printed by Miss Elliott for the choir and for the children of her father's church to teach them the truths of the Advent and Nativity season.

The tune name is MARGARET, composed especially for this text by Timothy R. Matthews (1826-1910). He was noted in Great Britain as one of the leading organists of his day along with his clergy position in the Church of England, serving one church for six years and another for 48 years. He composed 100 hymn tunes along with editing several hymn books.

This beautiful Christmas hymn is based on Luke 2:7, which reads, "there was no place for them in the inn." Notice the contrast of the first part of each stanza with the last section divided by the word "but." Christ had a wonderful situation in heaven, "but" he came to earth and experienced no room, the desert and great humiliation. In stanza five death is changed into victory. This is a Christmas hymn which deserves to be sung more often.

Scripture References: Matt. 8:20; Luke 2:1-7; John 1:11; 2 Cor. 8:9; Phil. 2:5-11; Heb. 1:2-8; 4:7

# In Christ There Is No East Or West

## *John Oxenham (1852-1941)*

*In Christ there is no east or west,*
*in him no south or north;*
*but one great fellowship of love*
*throughout the whole wide earth.*

*In Christ shall true hearts everywhere*
*their high communion find;*
*his service is the golden cord*
*close binding humankind.*

*In Christ is neither Jew nor Greek,*
*and neither slave nor free;*
*both male and female heirs are made,*
*and all are kin to me.*

*In Christ now meet both east and west,*
*in him meet south and north;*
*all Christly souls are one in him*
*throughout the whole wide earth.*

The text writer, John Oxenham, was born in Manchester, England, November 12, 1852. He received his college training at Victoria University. Unusual as it may seem, he used several different names. He was Arthur Dunkerly (his real name) for the wholesale grocery company which kept him traveling to branches in France, Canada and the United States. He was Julian Ross for fiction serial stories in the newspaper. For hymns and poems he was John Oxenham, which he took from the book *Western Ho*, given to him by his Sunday School teacher. The British *Who's Who* claims he took up writing "as an alternative from business and found it much more enjoyable." Along with business and writing, he was an active layman and deacon in the Euling Congregational Church in London.

The author's publishings include more than 40 novels and 20 books of verse and prose. His book *Hymns for the Men at the Front* sold eight million copies during the First World War. Later it was discovered that he had written 62 books using different names. This hymn text was found in his book *Bees in Amber*, which he printed himself in 1913 and sold 285,000 copies. The first American hymnal to include it was called *Hymns of the Living Age*, published by Augustine Smith in 1925.

The text was written in 1908 for a large missionary exhibit given by the London Missionary Society. It was thought that about a quarter of a million people saw it, which gave it so much publicity that it was used for several years (1908-1914) both in England and America.

Alexander Robert Reinagle (1799-1877) composed the tune ST. PETER, named for a church in Oxford, England, where Reinagle was organist for 31 years. His book *Psalm Tunes for the Voice and Pianoforte* (1836) included this tune. He wrote a sizeable amount of music which has a quality that is much liked by Christians of all cultures.

There is a story told about two ships that anchored side by side during World War II. One carried Japanese prisoners and the other, Americans waiting to be repatriated. For one day they stood along the railings glaring at each other. Finally someone began to sing "In Christ There Is No East or West." Shortly, those on the opposite ship joined in. A special chorus of former enemies were singing praises of Christ together. Hymns are truly a universal language.

Scripture References: Ps. 133:1; Rom. 12:5; 1 Cor. 12:12-13; Gal. 3:26-28; 5:13; Col. 3:11; 1 Peter 2:17

# Blest Be The Tie That Binds

## *John Fawcett (1740-1817)*

---

*Blest be the tie that binds our hearts in Christian love;
the fellowship of kindred minds is like to that above.*

*Before our Father's throne we pour our ardent prayers;
our fears, our hopes, our aims are one, our comforts and
our cares.*

*We share each other's woes, our mutual burdens bear;
and often for each other flows the sympathizing tear.*

*When we asunder part, it gives us inward pain;
but we shall still be joined in heart, and hope to meet
again.*

John Fawcett was born into a poor family at Lidget Green, Yorkshire, England, in 1740. At 16 years of age he dedicated his life to Christ and at 26 he was ordained a Baptist minister. His first church was at Wainsgate in West Yorkshire. Since the church was economically poor, his salary was quite low while his family was growing. Therefore he accepted a call from the influential Carter's Lane Baptist Church in London where the former well-known pastor had served 54 years.

When moving day arrived the sad parishioners hovered around the loaded wagons. Mrs. Fawcett finally cried out, "John, I cannot bear to leave. I know not how to go!" His reply was, "Nor can I either," so he gave the order to unpack the wagons.

In 1777 he started a school for young preachers and was offered a position as principal of the Baptist Academy at Bristol, which he turned down.

The Reverend Fawcett wrote poems for many years, and in 1782 he had a collection of 166 of them published under the title *Brotherly Love*. Books he wrote on practical Christianity also had a wide circulation. For his varied accomplishments he was awarded the Doctor of Divinity Degree by Brown University in 1811.

He faithfully remained with his Wainsgate parishioners until his death which was caused by a paralyzing stroke on July 25, 1817. John Fawcett's faithful life illustrated the spiritual tie that binds our hearts in Christian love.

Scripture References: Ps. 133:1; John 13:34-35; Rom. 12:5; 15:1-2; Gal. 3:28; 6:2; 1 Peter 3:8

# Just As I Am

## Charlotte Elliott (1789-1871)

*Just as I am, without one plea,*
*but that thy blood was shed for me,*
*and that thou bidst me come to thee,*

*Refrain:*
*O Lamb of God, I come, I come.*

*Just as I am, and waiting not*
*to rid my soul of one dark blot,*
*to thee whose blood can cleanse each spot,*

*Just as I am, though tossed about*
*with many a conflict, many a doubt,*
*fightings and fears within, without,*

*Just as I am, poor, wretched, blind;*
*sight, riches, healing of the mind,*
*yea, all I need in thee to find,*

*Just as I am, thou wilt receive,*
*wilt welcome, pardon, cleanse, relieve;*
*because thy promise I believe,*

*Just as I am, thy love unknown*
*hath broken every barrier down;*
*now, to be thine, yea, thine alone,*

This hymn has had greater influence on people and touched more souls to bring them into the Christian fold than any other. It came through suffering to song.

Charlotte Elliott's birthplace was Clapham, England, and the date was March 18, 1789. Her family were members of the church of England, many of them ministers. In her youth she showed artistic and literary talent when she painted portraits and wrote humorous poems. But her carefree life turned to sadness as her health failed, and by the age of 32 she was a permanently bed-ridden invalid.

In 1822 she met the Swiss preacher, Dr. Caesar Malan. Her life was transformed from feelings of despondency and despair to Christian service. She corresponded with Malan for 40 years, celebrating the date of their meeting as her soul's birthday. After his urging her to follow Christ, in resentment she responded, "But I do not know how to find Christ." He replied, "Come to Him just as you are."

Some years later (sources disagree on dates) when she was about 45, her brother, the Reverend H. V. Elliott, was raising funds to help start a college for the daughters of poor clergymen. A bazaar for this purpose was held at St. Mary's Hall, Brighton, and the Elliott family were busy working for it. As an invalid, Charlotte didn't know how she could help. Awake most of the night worrying, she lay on her couch feeling useless while the rest of the family were busy at the church. She thought of the Reverend Malan's words of years earlier to "come just as you are," which inspired the words of this hymn. She hoped the hymn might help her brother's worthy project. It brought in more funds than all of his projects and bazaars put together. He said, "I hoped to have been permitted to see some fruit of my labors, but I feel more has been done by a single hymn of my sister's." His words came true.

The hymn was first published in *The Invalid's Hymn Book* of 1834, which she edited. A woman who admired it reprinted it in leaflet form, evidently without Charlotte's name. A copy happened to come into the hands of her physician, so one day he gave it to her thinking it might give her comfort. To his great surprise he discovered he was presenting the poem to its author!

Charlotte Elliott wrote approximately 150 hymns, this being the first. Many of her religious poems appeared as *Hymns for a Week* and sold 40,000 copies. For 25 years she edited *The Christian Pocketbook*, a periodical where many of her hymns appeared.

After her death in 1871 at the age of 82, over 1,000 letters were discovered among her papers describing how much the hymn had helped their writers.

We can never know the vast number of lives changed through the use of this hymn since it has been sung regularly at the close of services in the renewal movements of two centuries. It reminds us of Jesus' words in John 6:37: "anyone who comes to me I will never drive away."

Scripture References: Ps. 51:1-2; Isa. 55:7; John 6:37; 2 Cor. 7:5; Eph. 2:13-14; Titus 3:5-6; 1 John 1:9; Rev. 22:17

# Come, Ye Thankful People, Come

## Henry Alford (1810-1871)

---

*Come, ye thankful people, come, raise the song of har-
vest home;*
*all is safely gathered in, ere the winter storms begin.*
*God our Maker doth provide for our wants to be
supplied;*
*come to God's own temple, come, raise the song of har-
vest home.*

*All the world is God's own field, fruit as praise to God
we yield;*
*wheat and tares together sown are to joy or sorrow
grown;*
*first the blade and then the ear, then the full corn shall
appear;*
*Lord of harvest, grant that we wholesome grain and pure
may be.*

*For the Lord our God shall come, and shall take the har-
vest home;*
*from the field shall in that day all offenses purge away,*
*giving angels charge at last in the fire the tares to cast;*
*but the fruitful ears to store in the garner evermore.*

*Even so, Lord, quickly come, bring thy final harvest
home;*
*gather thou thy people in, free from sorrow, free from
sin,*
*there, forever purified, in thy presence to abide;*
*come, with all thine angels, come, raise the glorious har-
vest home.*

This hymn was written for English harvest festivals held in various villages. The author, Henry Alford, was a very gifted Christian leader of the nineteenth century. London was the place of his birth on October 7, 1810. He came from a line of respected clergymen in the Church of England, and as a boy he decided to follow their examples. His ambition shows in what he wrote in his Bible when he was 16. "I do this day, in the presence of God and my own soul, renew my covenant with God, and solemnly determine henceforth to become His, and to do His work as far as in me lies."

He graduated from Trinity College, Cambridge, in 1832 and started his ministry in London. He held several positions before he was named Dean of Canterbury Cathedral, the leading church of England. From the age of 47 until his death, he remained in this prominent position, although he maintained good relations with nonconformist church groups such as Congregational and Baptist.

Dean Alford was known for his Greek scholarship. One of the century's standard commentaries, a four-volume edition of the Greek Testament, was the result of 20 years of work. As he was on the New Testament committee for the Revised Version, he made an important contribution to biblical scholarship in England and the United States.

One of the Reverend Alford's major interests was hymnology. He composed and translated many hymns which were published in his *Psalms and Hymns* (1844), *Poetical Works* (1852) and *The Year of Praise* (1867). This hymn, initially published in *Psalms and Hymns*, was first titled "After Harvest" and had seven stanzas.

In 1870 Henry Alford suffered a physical breakdown due to overwork. He died on January 12, 1871. He had always wanted to visit Jerusalem, but that dream never materialized in this world. So on his tombstone is the inscription, "The Inn of a Pilgrim Traveling to Jerusalem."

The composer of the tune is George J. Elvey who was organist 47 years for the historic royal chapel at Windsor Castle near London. It was originally written for another hymn but was found with Henry Alford's text in the Anglican Church hymnal called *Hymns Ancient and Modern*. Queen Victoria knighted George Elvey in 1871 for his music publications which, along with this tune (ST. GEORGE'S WINDSOR), included oratorios, anthems and other service music.

Plutarch wrote, "The worship most acceptable to God comes from a thankful and cheerful heart." It is said that after every meal and at the end of a day's work it was the practice of the Reverend Alford to give thanks to God. His hymn clearly reveals this gratitude.

Scripture References: Matt. 13:24-30, 36-43; Heb. 13:15; Rev. 14:15

# Jesus Calls Us

## Cecil Frances Alexander (1818-1895)

---

*Jesus calls us o'er the tumult*
*of our life's wild, restless sea;*
*day by day his sweet voice soundeth,*
*saying, "Christian, follow me!"*

*As of old the apostles heard it*
*by the Galilean lake,*
*turned from home and toil and kindred,*
*leaving all for Jesus' sake.*

*Jesus calls us from the worship*
*of the vain world's golden store,*
*from each idol that would keep us,*
*saying, "Christian, love me more!"*

*In our joys and in our sorrows,*
*days of toil and hours of ease,*
*still he calls, in cares and pleasures,*
*"Christian, love me more than these!"*

*Jesus calls us! By thy mercies,*
*Savior, may we hear thy call,*
*give our hearts to thine obedience,*
*serve and love thee best of all.*

In nineteenth century Ireland there were large numbers of poor farm workers. For several years following 1845 a serious famine spread over the country due to potatoes (their main crop) which rotted soon after they were harvested. Many

Irish people starved or fled the country. A young minister's wife, Cecil Frances Alexander, helped these people with food, clothing and some medical care.

When living on a farm in their early married life, her husband would come home in late afternoon and question her. "Have you sold the cow? Have you shown the gardener how to prune the roses? Have you finished writing that poem?" Once he read her a pamphlet written by an English minister which told of a great change in the heart and life of a man when he heard one of her hymns sung. Looking directly at him the usually humble poet said, "Thank God! I do like to hear that."

Cecil Frances Humphreys was born and raised in Ireland. As a little girl of nine years she liked to write poems, which were published in a small periodical that circulated within her family. Her father was a noted landowner who was also a major in the Royal Marines. They had a good family life. Her writing talent was noticeable at an early age, but her father was stern and critical of her work. So she hid her poems under the rug. One time he discovered them and, to her surprise, thought them quite good. He continued as time passed to encourage her.

As a young woman in her early twenties before her marriage, she was a member of the Anglican Church where she devoted her time to the religious education of children. She believed that teaching children the substance of Christian creeds and special Christian days is best accomplished through poetry. She wrote many hymns for her Sunday School students, reading the verses to them.

In 1846 when she was 21 she published her first book, *Verses for Holy Seasons*, which contained a hymn for every Sunday and other special days. The hymn "Jesus Calls Us" was used for St. Andrew's Day. Two years later another book called *Hymns For Little Children* appeared. This little book of 72 pages sold a quarter of a million copies in 20 years. By 1896 it reached its sixty-ninth edition.

The year of her marriage to the Reverend William Alexander was 1850. In their early married years, managing the farm took much of her time. She also made time to travel over miles of wet moorlands, mountains and bogs in all kinds of weather carrying food, warm clothing and medical supplies to the impoverished and sick of her husband's parish.

In one cottage she found a woman with a serious wound who had no one to care for her and no medical aid. Every day for six weeks she visited with the woman while she washed and dressed the wound until it was healed. Her life of service also included support of a Home for Fallen Women as well as speaking on child psychology.

Even though she had no children of her own, many of her hymns won their way into the hearts of the young. Two popular ones are "All Things Bright and Beautiful" and "Once in Royal David's City." "There is a Green Hill" was written for children also, but was so well liked by adults that it has been included in most adult hymnals.

Her writing of poetry continued until ten books were published containing about 400 hymns. Someone wrote that her hymns "are charmingly simple and tender, clear in dogma, and of poetic beauty." The great French composer Charles Gounod believed the hymn "Jesus Calls Us" to be near-perfect because of its simplicity. This was the only hymn she wrote for adults. It first appeared in a volume called *Hymns for Public Worship* (1852). This woman's beautiful hymn was adopted as the official hymn of the Brotherhood of St. Andrew of the Protestant Episcopal Church in the United States and the Church of England in Canada.

*The Gospel in Hymns* by Albert Edward Bailey has a good description of the writer's life. "She was admirably fitted to be a pastor's wife. She was as far as possible from the dreamy, ineffectual type of poet. She never posed, detested gush and sentimentality, had a direct tongue and incisive speech, and she turned a vigilant eye upon her husband's house, garden, and farm. She kept her devotional life largely hidden in her heart, but was a strict 'Prayer Book Christian,' going to church every day and to communion every week. Beyond that her days were largely given over to errands of charity and helpfulness, from one poor Irish home to another, from one sick-bed to another, from one house of sorrow to another, no matter how remote. She knew all her neighbors and loved them.''

When her husband became Bishop in 1867 and later Archbishop of Ireland, she was brought into contact with society and large Christian institutions. She was the hostess of many distinguished dignitaries and shared the publicity of her husband's prominent life. But she was as much at home in the impoverished areas as she was in the Archbishop's Palace, as his home was called.

It was in the palace that she died at the age of 72. Her funeral was at Londonderry, which was changed to Derry after Ireland's independence from England was gained in 1916. A great crowd gathered from England as well as Ireland, paying tribute to this noble woman.

"Jesus calls us o'er the tumult of our life's wild restless sea.'' In Ireland, they say you are never more than 60 miles from the sea. You would know how wild it could be but also how peaceful and calm it becomes. With Christ we can experience calm, even in the midst of tumult around us. As we sing we voice our prayer, "Give our hearts to thine obedience, serve and love thee best of all.''

Scripture References: Matt. 4:18-20; 10:37-38; 16:24; Luke 5:32; John 10:3-5, 27; 12:26; 21:15-17; 2 Tim. 1:9

# He Leadeth Me

## Joseph Henry Gilmore (1834-1918)

*He leadeth me: O blessed thought!*
*O words with heavenly comfort fraught!*
*Whate'er I do, where'er I be,*
*still 'tis God's hand that leadeth me.*

*Refrain:*
*He leadeth me, he leadeth me, by his own hand he leadeth*
*  me;*
*his faithful follower I would be, for by his hand he*
*  leadeth me.*

*Sometimes mid scenes of deepest gloom,*
*sometimes where Eden's bowers bloom,*
*by waters still, o'er troubled sea,*
*still 'tis his hand that leadeth me.*

*Lord, I would place my hand in thine,*
*nor ever murmur nor repine;*
*content, whatever lot I see,*
*since 'tis my God that leadeth me.*

*And when my task on earth is done,*
*when by thy grace the victory's won,*
*e'en death's cold wave I will not flee,*
*since God through Jordan leadeth me.*

Joseph Gilmore, author of "He Leadeth Me," was born in Boston, Massachusetts, in 1834 and later graduated with honors from Brown University as well as Newton Seminary.

He served as pastor of Baptist churches in New Hampshire and New York. He also taught Hebrew for a year at Rochester Seminary and spent two years as private secretary to his father, the governor of New Hampshire during the Civil War.

This hymn was written when Gilmore was 28 years old. He was invited to speak for two Sundays at the First Baptist Church of Philadelphia, Pennsylvania. At the midweek service he decided to give a study of the Twenty-Third Psalm, which he had used on other occasions, but this time he did not get beyond the words "He leadeth me."

The country was in the "darkest hour" of the Civil War. He believed it may have subconsciously led him to realize that "God's leadership is the one significant fact in human experience, that it makes no difference how we are led, or whether we are led, so long as we are sure that God is leading us." At the close of the service Gilmore with a few others went to the home of his host. There they continued the discussion of divine guidance as he wrote the words of this hymn. He handed the paper to his wife, who had come with him on this speaking trip, and forgot about it.

Three years later he traveled to Rochester, New York, to preach a trial sermon at the Second Baptist Church. "I picked up a church hymnal to see what songs they sang and was surprised to have the book fall open to the very song I had written three years earlier. To me," he said, "this was an indication of divine leadership with regard to my acceptance of this pastorate."

When he returned home he talked to his wife about the poem and asked her how it could have been set to music and put into the hymnbook when he had not given it to anybody. His wife smiled and said, "I can explain it, Joseph. I felt that the words would bless the hearts of people in those troublesome times, so I sent the poem to *The Watchman and Reflector*. I am glad to know that they have printed it." Dr. Bradbury read the poem in the magazine and thought that it should be set to music. He did so, added the last two lines of the refrain and had it published in his 1864 book *Golden Censer*.

William Bradbury (1816-1868) was a native of York, Maine. After he studied music in Boston he became an organist and choirmaster. A story was told about his problem as organist in his first church, which was small and offered him $25 a year. When he began the job he found that the church organ needed the musician to depress the keys, then pull up to stop the sound. So he asked that his pay be doubled, since his work was doubled. Fortunately, he went on to better things and contributed much to church and choral music in America. He published about 59 hymn books.

This reminds us of Psalm 23. It shows how God leads us all through our lives and even through death. When we clasp hands with Christ we are led until, by grace, the victory's won.

Scripture References: Ps. 23; 48:14; 73:23-24; 139:1-12; Isa. 41:13; 48:17

# For All The Saints

## *William Walsham How (1823-1897)*

*For all the saints, who from their labors rest,*
*who thee by faith before the world confessed,*
*thy name, O Jesus, be forever blest.*

*Refrain:*
*Alleluia, alleluia!*

*Thou wast their rock, their fortress, and their might;*
*thou, Lord, their captain in the well-fought fight;*
*thou, in the darkness drear, their one true light.*

*O may thy soldiers, faithful, true, and bold,*
*fight as the saints who nobly fought of old,*
*and win with them the victor's crown of gold.*

*O blest communion, fellowship divine!*
*We feebly struggle, they in glory shine;*
*yet all are one in thee, for all are thine.*

*And when the strife is fierce, the warfare long,*
*steals on the ear the distant triumph song,*
*and hearts are brave again, and arms are strong.*

*From earth's wide bounds, from ocean's farthest coast,*
*through gates of pearl streams in the countless host,*
*singing to Father, Son, and Holy Ghost:*

This hymn was written by William Walsham How, who
was born into a wealthy Anglican Church family and educated at Oxford. One of the most loved bishops in the Church of

England, he gave his entire life in sacrificial service to God. He was called the "omnibus bishop" because he rode a bus instead of the private coach he could afford.

After a number of years as a minister, he became the bishop of East London, a poverty area with the worst social conditions. Due to his pastoral devotion and warmhearted humanity, he became known as "the people's bishop," "the poor man's bishop," and "the children's bishop." He liked the last name the best, since he always felt comfortable in the company of children. The Reverend Barnett, a well-known social worker in the East London area, wrote of the bishop when How left. "With the people he was distinctly the most popular man in East London; the one person among the crowd of rival politicians and philanthropists whom they thoroughly trusted." At age 65, after declining a number of important bishoprics, he left East London to become bishop of Wakefield for the remainder of his life.

Bishop How was a great hymn lover. He collaborated with others in editing two hymnals, and in 1886 he published a volume of his own *Poems and Hymns.* Concerning this interest he said, "A good hymn is something like a good prayer — simple, real, earnest, and reverent." His own hymns filled these requirements. He wrote about 60, of which 25 are still in use today. Most standard hymnals include eight to twelve of his hymns. Other best known ones are "O Word of God Incarnate," "O Jesus, Thou Art Standing," and "We Give Thee But Thine Own."

All of his 60 hymns were written while the Reverend How was rector at Whittington, a pleasant farming village on the Welsh border. Opposite the church is a castle built by the Normans to keep out Welsh raiders. Being a wealthy man, How rebuilt and enlarged the rectory, laid out extensive gardens and lawns (including an archery range), planted trees, built barns and cultivated large amounts of land. He also rebuilt the church which had deteriorated for a century and a half.

After Bishop How died on April 10, 1879, while vacationing in Ireland, he was buried in the churchyard he had earlier

111

improved. The monument which once stood over the grave has been moved across the road and is known as How's Cross.

"For All the Saints" was published in *Hymns for Saints' Days and Other Hymns* (1864). It has been described as "praised by the best critics, accepted by the highest authorities, and introduced in nearly all compilations over the world." It is a commentary on the clause of the Apostles' Creed, "I believe in the Communion of Saints." Its eleven stanzas have been edited down to six or seven. It is the finest of all hymns written for All Saints' Day because it contains more of the purely spiritual element and less of pageantry. An outline for it can be by verse numbers:

1. Our thanks to Jesus for the saints.
2. He was their inspiration and strength.
3. May we prove worthy of them.
4. Even now we have fellowship with them in spirit.
5. Memories of their victories strengthen us.
6. After the fight comes rest.
7. But our true reward will come in the great review above, in which we all will assemble to praise God.

Scripture References: Acts 20:32; 1 Thess. 4:13-17; Heb. 4:9; 11:13-16; 1 Peter 1:3-5; Rev. 14:13

# More Love To Thee, O Christ

## Elizabeth Payson Prentiss (1818-1878)

*More love to thee, O Christ, more love to thee!*
*Hear thou the prayer I make on bended knee.*
*This is my earnest plea: More love, O Christ, to thee;*
*more love to thee, more love to thee!*

*Once earthly joy I craved, sought peace and rest;*
*now thee alone I seek, give what is best.*
*This all my prayer shall be: More love, O Christ, to thee;*
*more love to thee, more love to thee!*

*Let sorrow do its work, come grief and pain;*
*sweet are thy messengers, sweet their refrain,*
*when they can sing with me: More love, O Christ, to thee;*
*more love to thee, more love to thee!*

*Then shall my latest breath whisper thy praise;*
*this be the parting cry my heart shall raise;*
*this still its prayer shall be: More love, O Christ, to thee;*
*more love to thee, more love to thee!*

The author of this hymn, Elizabeth Payson Prentiss, came from one of the oldest families in New England. Her father, Edward Payson, was descended from the original Edward Payson, a native of Essex, England, who came to America in 1635 and settled in Roxbury, Massachusetts. When she was born on October 26, 1818, her family lived in Portland, Maine.

Her father was a highly gifted and spiritual man who had wide influence. After he died hundreds of boys all over the

113

United States were named for him. Elizabeth later wrote, "I once saw the deaths of three Edward Paysons in one paper." All through her childhood she regarded her father very highly, and to the end of her life she could remember the smallest details about him even though he died when she was only nine.

Under the supervision of her older sister, Elizabeth laid the foundation of a careful education. She showed much intelligence along with a deeply religious character. When she was 16 she began having some of her poetry and prose published in the magazine *Youth's Companion*. For four years she taught in young women's seminaries in Richmond, Virginia, and in Maine.

She continued to teach in Massachusetts until she married George Prentiss, pastor of the Congregational Church in New Bedford. After the couple spent two years in Europe, he became a minister in New York City where they lived the rest of their lives. George was a professor of Homiletics and Polity at Union Theological Seminary.

Elizabeth suffered all of her life from chronic headaches and insomnia. She wanted to be cheerful to people, so she very seldom mentioned her condition. In fact, she was described as "a bright-eyed little lady with a sense of humor." She preferred to be at home instead of going out to social events.

During her second year in New York, two of her three children died within a few weeks' time. After her death a scrap of paper was found in her desk on which were these penciled words:

> *I thought that prattling boys and girls*
> *Would fill this empty room;*
> *That my rich heart would gather flowers*
> *From childhood's opening bloom.*
> *One child and two green graves are mine;*
> *This is God's gift to me:*
> *A bleeding, fainting, broken heart —*
> *This is my gift to Thee.*

After returning home from putting flowers on the graves of their children, Elizabeth cried out to her husband, "Our home is broken up, our lives wrecked, our hopes shattered, our dreams dissolved. Sometimes I don't think I can stand living for another moment, much less a lifetime." He held her close and let her cry. Then he very quietly said, "In times like these, God loves us all the more, just as we loved our children in their distress."

Once when her husband was gone she was having her devotions, reading scripture and the hymn "Nearer, My God, to Thee" by Sarah Adams. As she prayed, the words of "More Love to Thee, O Christ" came to mind. She wrote them down, but nobody knew about her poem, not even her husband, until 13 years later.

In the meantime she began creating books for children. She continued until she had written a large amount of literature. Her children's books, some in a series, became classics of their time. *Golden Hours* (1873) was a collection of original hymns and devotional poems. Her most popular work, *Stepping Heavenward*, was autobiographical and came out the same year as this hymn (1856). This book was written to strengthen and comfort others, and more than 150,000 copies were sold in this country. It was also translated for several other countries, meeting with wide circulation and high praise. It has recently been republished.

When Elizabeth Prentiss died on August 13, 1878, at her summer home in Dorset, Vermont, people around the world mourned. Even from China a fan was received with her hymn inscribed in beautiful Chinese characters. Soon after her death, her husband published a biography of her called *Life and Letters*. In it he tells the story of this popular hymn's birth. He writes, "Like most of her hymns, it is simply a prayer put into the form of verse. She wrote it so hastily that the last stanza was left incomplete, one line having to be added in pencil when it was printed. She did not show it, not even to her husband, until many years after it was written; and she wondered not a little that, when published, it met with so much favor."

The tune was composed by William Doane (1832-1915), who was born in Connecticut but later lived in Cincinnati, Ohio. He was a successful businessman who began to write hymn tunes as an avocation after he was stricken with a serious illness in 1862. He composed over 2,000 melodies for hymns, many of them for Fanny Crosby. This tune was found in his 1870 book, one of his 40 collections.

As we sing of our love for Christ we can remember Elizabeth Prentiss's words: "To love Christ more is the deepest need, the constant cry of my soul ... out in the woods, and on my bed, and out driving, when I am happy and busy, and when I am sad and idle, the whisper keeps going up for more love, more love, more love!"

Scripture References: Deut. 6:5; Phil. 1:9; 2 Thess. 3:5; 1 John 4:19

# Take My Life

## *Frances Ridley Havergal (1836-1879)*

---

*Take my life, and let it be consecrated, Lord, to thee.*
*Take my moments and my days; let them flow in cease-*
*less praise.*
*Take my hands, and let them move at the impulse of thy*
*love.*
*Take my feet, and let them be swift and beautiful for thee.*

*Take my voice, and let me sing always, only, for my King.*
*Take my lips, and let them be filled with messages from*
*thee.*
*Take my silver and my gold; not a mite would I withhold.*
*Take my intellect, and use every power as thou shalt*
*choose.*

*Take my will, and make it thine; it shall be no longer*
*mine.*
*Take my heart, it is thine own; it shall be thy royal throne.*
*Take my love, my Lord, I pour at thy feet its*
*treasure-store.*
*Take myself, and I will be ever, only, all for thee.*

Born in Astley, Worcestershire, England, on December 14, 1836, Miss Frances Ridley Havergal experienced the death of her mother when she was four years old. At 14 she entered a special Christian school where the influences were helpful. The following year she said, "I committed my soul to the Savior, and earth and heaven seemed brighter from that moment."

She was also influenced by her father, William Havergal, who was a musician and hymn writer as well as a clergyman in the Church of England. He wrote tunes to be used with her hymns and had two books published. One was called *The Old Church Psalmody, History of the Old Hundredth Tune* (the Doxology). The other book was a collection of 100 original hymn tunes.

Frances's father called her "Little Quicksilver" as she was very bright, learning to read at the age of four. In her girlhood she memorized the complete New Testament, Psalms and Isaiah. She showed early promise for an unusual career as a linguist, speaking Latin, Greek, Hebrew, French, German and Italian.

Her outstanding musical abilities included classical performance on piano as well as vocal and composition. People especially enjoyed hearing her play the Beethoven "Moonlight Sonata." But instead of concert performance she turned to "love and service for God," which were her high ideals.

Along with writing hymns she wrote many letters, leaflets and books. She taught Sunday School, conducted religious meetings and made public addresses. The work she felt was demanded of her gradually broke her health and wore down her spirit. She said she hoped "the angels would have orders to let her alone a bit when she first got to heaven." She apparently enjoyed some recreation, for in one of her books she tells how she went hiking and skiing in the Swiss Alps.

She said concerning her poems, which filled six volumes (over 65 hymns), that they came to her without effort. She believed that her talents were a trust from God and were to be used accordingly. To her, writing was the same as praying. Giving the credit to God, she said, "I can never set myself to write verse. I believe my King suggests a thought, ... whispers me a musical line or two, ... I look up, ... thank God delightedly and go on with it."

Her first notable hymn was "I Gave My Life for Thee," written in 1857 when she was about 21. While visiting in Germany, she had entered a minister's study. Feeling tired, she sat down as she looked at a painting of Christ on the cross. The caption read, "I did this for thee; what hast thou done for me?" As she gazed at the Redeemer, the lines of the hymn came to mind; so taking a pencil she wrote them on the back of a leaflet. When she read them over, she thought they so poorly expressed her feelings that she lamented, "This is not poetry," and threw it into the fire. But immediately something compelled her to rescue it, which she did, stuffing the singed paper into her pocket.

Later she made a call on an old woman in the poorhouse. Frances began to talk to her, as she always did, about her Savior. She wondered if the woman would care for her verses, which she felt sure nobody else would care to read. So she read them to the woman, who was so delighted with them that when Frances went home she copied them. Her father, after composing a tune for her text, had it published two years later, and now it is her most widely known hymn.

"Take My Life" was written on the evening of February 4, 1874, when she was 38. A group of ten people were gathered for a going-away party in honor of another hymn writer. During the evening Frances studied each member there and observed that the happiest of the group were those who had found their respective places in life and were using their talents accordingly. After the guests had gone the poetess retired to her room. She was ill that night as she had been most of her short life. But she began to write and by dawn she had completed the hymn.

Frances Havergal wanted her hymns to be sung with her father's tunes. Once she wrote, "I was so overwhelmed on Sunday at hearing three of my hymns touchingly sung in Perry Church. I never before realized the high privilege of writing for the great congregation, especially when they sang 'I Gave My Life' to my father's tune." "Take My Life" was also to be sung with her father's tune, but hymnal editors overlooked the author's request. In 1930 a study was made of 25 hymnals in England and America. Fourteen different tunes were found with her text of this hymn.

When visiting her physician at age 42, Miss Havergal was told that her health problems were serious and that she did not have long to live. She replied, "If I am really going, it is too good to be true." At the bottom of her bed where she could easily see it was the Bible verse "The blood of Jesus His Son cleanses us from all sin."

Shortly before her death on Whit Tuesday, June 3, 1879, she finished revising the proofs of *Kept for the Master's Use*. This beautiful little devotional book (including pictures) was taken from this hymn. Her sister had the book published the following autumn. The 13 chapters are about keeping our lives for Jesus: our moments, our hands, our feet, our voices, our lips, our silver and gold, our intellects, our wills, our hearts, our love, our selves. In the last chapter she reminds us of "the love of Christ that passeth knowledge."

Scripture References: 1 Chron. 29:5; Matt. 22:37; Rom. 6:13; 12:1; 1 Cor. 6:19-20; 2 Tim. 2:20-21

# Break Thou The Bread Of Life

## Mary A. Lathbury (1841-1913)

*Break thou the bread of life, dear Lord, to me,*
*as thou didst break the loaves beside the sea;*
*beyond the sacred page I seek thee, Lord;*
*my spirit pants for thee, O Living Word!*

*Bless thou the truth, dear Lord, to me, to me,*
*as thou didst bless the bread by Galilee;*
*then shall all bondage cease, all fetters fall;*
*and I shall find my peace, my all in all.*

August 10, 1841, was the birth date of Mary Artemisia Lathbury. Several of her family were Methodist ministers, including her father and two brothers. Her birthplace was Manchester, New York.

Near Jamestown, New York, is the beautiful Lake Chautauqua. The Methodists began Chautauqua as a two-week summer camp meeting. Through the years it has broadened to last all summer and include cultural, literary and spiritual activities. In 1877, a few years after she helped to found Chautauqua, Mary Lathbury served there as private secretary for Bishop John H. Vincent.

Mary had many talents, first as an artist when she taught art in the schools of Vermont and New York. She also became involved in Christian work and in writing. She recalled later that in her youth she heard God's voice encouraging her. "Remember my child that you have a gift of weaving fancies

121

(words) into verse and a gift with the pencil of producing visions that come to your heart: consecrate these talents to Me as thoroughly and as definitely as you do your inmost spirit."

Miss Lathbury liked to paint pictures of children, and in 1898 a popular book she wrote for children called *The Child's Story of the Bible* was published. She was assistant editor of several papers and founded a club for children called "Look-up Legion," which attracted more than 4,000 boys and girls to the church. Frances E. Willard, the Christian temperance leader, wrote of her, "She had a high courageous faith, a loyalty to the best ideals, and a devotion to the truth that gave inspiration to all with whom she came in contact."

At Chautauqua in the summer of 1877, the bishop asked Miss Lathbury to write two hymns, one for a Bible study and one for a vesper service. As she sat beside the beautiful lake, she prayed for guidance with regard to her assignment. She thought of the 5,000 at Galilee and prayed, "Dear Lord, break thou the bread of life to me as thou didst break the loaves beside the sea." Thus the words of her Bible study hymn poured forth. Later, as the sun began to set over the lake, she felt moved to write the first two stanzas of the vesper hymn, "Day Is Dying in the West." For her work she became known as "Poet Laureate of Chautauqua."

The tunes for these two texts were also composed at Chautauqua by the director of music, William Fisk Sherwin (1826-1888), who was lovable, witty, and devout. Sherwin was a professor at the New England Conservatory of Music in Boston. Another Christian musician, George Stebbins, was there when "Day is Dying in the West" was first sung. Describing the experience he wrote, "On Saturday evening in August, about 2,000 people gathered on the shores of Lake Chautauqua. On the water near the shore was a boat in which were the professor and I. About this central boat were 30 other little boats filled with men, women and children. It was a beautiful scene and a very impressive sight as we sang this lovely hymn together."

The two stanzas of Mary Lathbury's "Break Thou the Bread of Life" make it one of the shortest hymns in the English language. Its 71 words take about 75 seconds to sing at a moderate tempo. The phrase "beside the sea" suggests the place where Jesus was and where the hymn was first sung. "The bread of life" gives the purpose of the Bible study, which is to be spiritually fed. As we sing this hymn we think of Christ our Living Word, who is just as present with us today as he was many years ago in Galilee.

Scripture References: Deut. 8:3; Jer. 15:16; Matt. 4:4; 14:15-21; Luke 24:32, 45; John 6:35
St. 1   John 5:39
St. 2   Ps. 119:44-45; John 8:32

# O Master, Let Me Walk With Thee

## Washington Gladden (1836-1918)

---

O Master, let me walk with thee in lowly paths of service
free;
tell me thy secret; help me bear the strain of toil, the fret
of care.

Help me the slow of heart to move by some clear, win-
ning word of love;
teach me the wayward feet to stay, and guide them in
the homeward way.

Teach me thy patience; still with thee in closer, dearer
company,
in work that keeps faith sweet and strong, in trust that
triumphs over wrong;

In hope that sends a shining ray far down the future's
broadening way,
in peace that only thou canst give, with thee, O Master,
let me live.

Washington Gladden was born on a farm in Potts Grove,
Pennsylvania, on February 11, 1836. He studied at Oswego
Academy where he learned the printer's trade. He graduated
from Williams College in 1859 and was ordained to the ministry
in the Congregational Church, holding several pastorates in
the East. While serving in Springfield, Massachusetts, he edited
a paper called *Sunday Afternoon*, where this hymn was first
published in 1879.

The Civil War had been fought in the 1860s, and there was much emphasis at that time on Christianity's implications for this nation. Many ministers including the Reverend Gladden became enthusiastic leaders for the cause of social justice. Gladden spent much of his career fighting political groups.

In 1882 he was called to the First Congregational Church of Columbus, Ohio, where he stayed for 32 years. While living in Columbus he became one of the most powerful pulpit voices in America. It has been written that he applied "the gospel to the social, political and economic life of America and the world." Known for his activities in various national disputes or strikes, he thought that the duty of the Christian Church was to "elevate the masses" not only spiritually and morally, but to be concerned also about their social and economic welfare. For these views he was the object of much criticism throughout his life.

This text was written as a devotional meditation to be printed in his paper under the title "Walking With God." When it was suggested that it be used as a hymn, Gladden chose the tune MARYTON to be sung with it. The composer was Anglican minister Henry Percy Smith (1825-1898). The tune had been used with other texts, and this text has been used with other tunes. (In the late 1800s there were some hymn books with all the pages cut in half horizontally. The music was on one half and the words on the other so people could choose which tunes and texts they wanted together.)

Washington Gladden died in 1918. He was widely known in his day for his strong preaching and writing, but he is best remembered today for this one hymn. It reflects some of the struggle of that day. A few lines are no longer in the text.

*O Master let me walk with thee*
*Before the taunting Pharisee;*
*Help me to bear the sting of spite,*
*The hate of men who hide thy light.*

*The sore distrust of souls sincere*
*Who cannot read thy judgments clear,*

*The dullness of the multitude*
*Who dimly guess that thou art good.*

Concerning the hymn he wrote, "It had no liturgical purpose and no theological significance, but it was an honest cry of human need, need of divine companionship."

Scripture References: Matt. 20:26-28; Luke 6:40; John 12:26; 13:13-14; Gal. 5:13; Eph. 2:10; Col. 1:10; 2 Thess. 2:17; Heb. 12:1; James 1:22; 1 John 2:6

# O Love That Wilt Not Let Me Go

## George Matheson (1842-1906)

---

*O Love that wilt not let me go,*
*I rest my weary soul in thee;*
*I give thee back the life I owe,*
*that in thine ocean depths its flow may richer, fuller be.*

*O Light that followest all my way,*
*I yield my flickering torch to thee;*
*my heart restores its borrowed ray,*
*that in thy sunshine's blaze its day may brighter, fairer be.*

*O Joy that seekest me through pain,*
*I cannot close my heart to thee;*
*I trace the rainbow thru the rain,*
*and feel the promise is not vain, that morn shall tearless*
*be.*

*O Cross that liftest up my head,*
*I dare not ask to fly from thee;*
*I lay in dust life's glory dead,*
*and from the ground there blossoms red life that shall*
*endless be.*

George Matheson was a blind hymn writer. He was born March 27, 1842, in Glasgow, Scotland. In his childhood he could barely see, but he pretended he was a preacher. His father had been a minister and later changed to business. By the time he entered the University of Glasgow in 1857, George was completely blind. This did not deter him from excelling as the best student in the school.

Matheson never married since the one he loved could not accept his blindness. His intellectual family members encouraged and supported him, especially one sister whose name we do not know. She gave her life to him, learning Greek, Latin and Hebrew as she took four years of theological studies. His college essays are in her handwriting. She stayed with him throughout his life and spent much of her time reading to him. He leaned on her and it was his greatest dread that she should die before he did, but that did not happen.

With a scholar's instinct and ambitions, his life would be very difficult because of his handicap. But he turned his problem over to God. He stood the test of faith and found the Christian secret of submission and self-surrender that we sing about in this hymn. He could paint beautiful word pictures. In one of his student sermons he said, "Death is the gate to higher work and purer joys. The fruits ripen every year ... but what person ever came to full maturity ... Life, long or short, is but a waiting to be born into a sphere, and death is the birth-angel."

His family vacationed at two seaside resorts where he liked to go boating and enjoy the beauty of both land and sea even though he was blind. Most of his "sacred songs" were written in those summers while he was a student at Glasgow University. After license for the ministry in the Church of Scotland was given him in June of 1866, his first parish was Innellan, which was another summer seaside retreat. There was strong opposition to a blind minister, but he soon won the hearts of the people, proved a capable pastor, and stayed there for 18 years.

Matheson became known as a preacher of very unusual power, even for Scotland, the land of great preachers. During the summer season he had two Sunday services for the many people who vacationed in Innellan so they could hear him. He dictated his sermons in full to his sister and had her read them back to him a few times before he preached them from memory. She continued to help him in all his pastoral duties.

At Innellan he wrote this hymn which was composed in a few minutes and the only popular hymn he ever wrote. But his whole personality and deepest experiences are behind the hymn. It is the high point of his career as a writer. He said, "Its writing was a unique experience" for he had "no natural gift of rhythm. All the other verses were manufactured articles; this came like a dayspring from on high." He said he had "never been able to gain once more the same fervor in verse." He writes:

> My hymn was composed in the manse of Innellan on the evening of 6th June, 1882. I was at that time alone. It was the day of my sister's marriage, and the rest of the family were staying over night in Glasgow. Something had happened to me, which was known only to myself, and which caused me the most severe mental suffering. The hymn was the fruit of that suffering. It was the quickest bit of work I ever did in my life. I had the impression rather of having it dictated to me by some inward voice than of working it out myself. I am quite sure that the whole work was completed in five minutes, and equally sure that it never received at my hands any retouching or correction. The Hymnal committee of the Church of Scotland desired the change of one word. I had written originally "I climb the rainbow in the rain." They objected to the word "climb" and I put in "trace."

The hymn was first published in the Church of Scotland magazine, *Life and Work*, in January of 1883.

One of the several books Dr. Matheson wrote had some defects which critics strongly pointed out. A friend later wrote, "When he saw that for the purposes of scholarship his blindness was a fatal hindrance, he withdrew from the field — not without pangs, but finally." Matheson himself wrote, "My life has been a life that has beaten persistently against the cage of circumstances and at the time of abandoned work has said not 'Good night,' but 'Good morning.' " He tried higher biblical criticism, which discouraged him, so he retired within his own soul to renew the fires of faith and deepen the inner life of communion with God. His later books are expository and devotional, glowing and deeply spiritual, like a prophet seeing the invisible and trying to describe his vision.

Before he left Innellan he had the honor of being summoned to preach before Queen Victoria. She wrote afterwards that she was "immensely delighted with the sermon and the prayers." Instead of the customary signed photograph, she gave him a little carved figurine of herself.

In 1886 at age 44 he was installed as minister of St. Bernard's Parish Church in Edinburgh with some 2,000 members. Here he repeated his earlier success and became a light to the community. He was especially noted for his public prayers. A contemporary wrote, "Though his visual sight is entirely eclipsed, he does 'see God,' and he does see into the souls of hearers. In that prayer we have been to the mount of worship."

In 1890 Dr. Matheson gathered together a collection of his hymns and published them in a book called *Sacred Songs*. He continued at the last parish for 13 years until the work became too heavy. His last years were spent preparing more books and preaching. He died August 28, 1906.

The theme of the hymn is the parables of the Lost Sheep and the Lost Coin, or the pursuit of the human soul by the Spirit of God. Like the lost sheep we are ready to be found and to receive Christ's love, so we sing about the love that will not let us go, the light that follows all our way, and the joy that seeks us through pain.

Scripture References: Jer. 31:3; John 12:32; 15:9-11
St. 1   Rom. 8:35-39; Eph. 3:17-19
St. 2   2 Sam. 22:29; Ps. 36:9; John 8:12
St. 3   Ps. 16:11; Rom. 15:13
St. 4   Gal. 6:14

# Lead On, O King Eternal

## *Ernest W. Shurtleff (1862-1917)*

---

*Lead on, O King eternal, the day of march has come;*
*henceforth in fields of conquest thy tents shall be our*
*home.*
*Through days of preparation thy grace has made us*
*strong;*
*and now, O King eternal, we lift our battle song.*

*Lead on, O King eternal, till sin's fierce war shall cease,*
*and holiness shall whisper the sweet amen of peace.*
*For not with swords loud clashing, nor roll of stirring*
*drums;*
*with deeds of love and mercy the heavenly kingdom*
*comes.*

*Lead on, O King eternal, we follow, not with fears,*
*for gladness breaks like morning where'er thy face*
*appears.*
*Thy cross is lifted o'er us, we journey in its light;*
*the crown awaits the conquest; lead on, O God of might.*

Born in Boston, Massachusetts, on April 4, 1862, Ernest W. Shurtleff had a natural poetic ability. Therefore, when he was a student at Andover Seminary he was asked to write a new graduation song to fit the popular tune LANCASHIRE by Henry Smart (his story is with "Angels From the Realms of Glory"). Smart composed it for the three-hundredth anniversary of the Reformation in England. Lancashire is the place where Smart was organist. This tune has been used by many countries and with many sets of words.

At the time of his graduation from Andover Seminary, Shurtleff, a graduate of Harvard University, had already published two books of poetry. This hymn was written especially for their commencement service of 1887. He went from seminary graduation to serve churches in California, Michigan, and Massachusetts. He also traveled abroad to establish the American Church at Frankfurt, Germany. In 1906 he and his wife moved to Paris to direct the student activities of an academy. For his contributions in music and preaching, he was awarded the honorary degree Doctor of Divinity by Ripon College. He did some relief work during World War I and died in Paris in 1917.

This hymn of consecration is appropriate for any seminary graduation. In the first stanza we sing about "days of preparation" and "fields of conquest." The second stanza brings out the futility of war or "swords loud clashing." In the third stanza we hear of courage and optimism when we follow Christ, "not with fears." "Gladness breaks like morning" when "Thy cross is lifted o'er us." When the "God of might" leads us, a "crown awaits the conquest."

The hymn appeals to youth who face the unknown future as a great opportunity for service. We hear a strong belief that enlightenment, justice and good will are moving forward as there is a steady advance of God's Kingdom on earth. It sounds the wholehearted committal of mind, soul, and body to the guidance of Jesus Christ.

Scripture References: Isa. 48:17; Eph. 6:10-20; 1 Tim. 6:12; 2 Tim. 2:3-4; 4:7-8; Jude 3; Rev. 17:14
St. 1   2 Cor. 12:9
St. 2   1 Cor. 15:56-58
St. 3   Gal. 6:14; 2 Tim. 4:8; Rev. 2:10

# Open My Eyes That I May See

## *Clara H. Scott (1841-1897)*

---

*Open my eyes, that I may see glimpses of truth thou hast
    for me;*
*place in my hands the wonderful key that shall unclasp
    and set me free.*

*Refrain:*
*Silently now I wait for thee, ready, my God, thy will to
    see.*
*Open my eyes (my ears; my heart), illumine me, Spirit
    divine!*

*Open my ears, that I may hear voices of truth thou send-
    est clear;*
*and while the wavenotes fall on my ear, everything false
    will disappear.*

*Open my mouth, and let me bear gladly the warm truth
    everywhere;*
*open my heart and let me prepare love with thy children
    thus to share.*

Clara H. Scott, who wrote both the words and music of this hymn, was born Clara Jones on December 3, 1841, in Elk Grove, Illinois. Her musical family lived in a Chicago suburb. She was 15 when she began her study of composition at the first music institute held in Chicago. In 1857 she began teaching music at the Ladies' Seminary in Lyons, Iowa.

Three years later she married Henry Clay Scott and continued her musical activities in Chicago. After she met another musician, Horatio R. Palmer, she began composing anthems which were published in a collection called *Royal Anthem Book* in 1882. It was the first book of anthems by a woman and became popular. Another collection which included this hymn was *Truth in Song*, released in the fall of 1897 after her tragic death.

The people of Dubuque, Iowa, were stunned when they read the paper on June 22, 1897. It told of an accident caused by a runaway horse. In a two-seated carriage were three women who had just attended the funeral of a former classmate. Clara had come back to Dubuque from Chicago to be present at the service. On a sharp incline the horse grew so frightened that it became unmanageable. Two of the women were killed instantly in the wreck. Clara Scott, one of these women, was 56 years old. She could never know how popular her hymn became. We sing it today as a lasting memorial and prayer of enlightenment.

Scripture References: Ps. 40:8; Prov. 20:12; Ezek. 36:27; Matt. 13:16; Mark 8:18; Col. 1:9; 1 John 5:6
St. 1  Ps. 119:18; John 8:32
St. 2  Prov. 4:20; 15:31; Matt. 11:15
St. 3  Ps. 49:3; Rom. 5:5; Eph. 4:15

# I Would Be True

*Howard Arnold Walter (1883-1918)*

---

*I would be true, for there are those who trust me;*
*I would be pure, for there are those who care;*
*I would be strong, for there is much to suffer;*
*I would be brave, for there is much to dare;*
*I would be brave, for there is much to dare.*

*I would be friend of all the foe, the friendless;*
*I would be giving, and forget the gift;*
*I would be humble, for I know my weakness;*
*I would look up, and laugh, and love, and lift;*
*I would look up, and laugh, and love, and lift.*

*I would be learning day by day the lessons*
*My heav'nly Father gives me in his Word;*
*I would be quick to hear his lightest whisper,*
*And prompt and glad to do the things I've heard;*
*And prompt and glad to do the things I've heard.*

*I would be prayerful through each busy moment;*
*I would be constantly in touch with God;*
*I would be tuned to hear his slightest whisper;*
*I would have faith to keep the path Christ trod;*
*I would have faith to keep the path Christ trod.*

Born August 19, 1883, in New Britain, Connecticut, Howard Arnold Walter graduated from Princeton University in 1905 with scholastic honors. He spent the following year in Japan teaching English at Waseda University where he wrote

135

this poem on July 1, 1906. It was first titled "My Creed" and included three stanzas. He sent it home to his mother, Mrs. Henry S. Walter. She thought it was a rich message that should not be confined to the family. So she sent it to *Harper's Magazine* where it was published in May, 1907. Later, in 1928, he wrote the fourth verse.

Following more study at Hartford Theological Seminary and universities in Edinburgh, Glasgow and Gottingen, Mr. Walter was ordained to the ministry at the Asylum Avenue Congregational Church in Hartford, Connecticut.

In 1912 he went to India for the Young Men's Christian Association. A specialist warned him of his bad heart, but he thought it better to keep working. He died during an influenza epidemic on November 1, 1918, eight years after his ordination and six years after he began his missionary work among the Muslim students at Foreman Christian College in Lahore, India. His last words were, "O Christ, I am ready." In this hymn Howard Walter has left the Christian world a rich legacy and challenge.

Scripture References: Acts 11:23; 1 Cor. 16:13-14; Eph. 4:1-3; 1 Tim. 4:12; 1 Peter 3:8

# Appendix

## A Concise History Of Hymnology

Songs of praise to God are among our earliest available writings. The singing of hymns was the largest section of the old Egyptian ritual. Four times a day — at sunrise, noon, sunset, and midnight — the priests sang praises regularly to their gods. Moses may have become familiar with these hymns since he was given an Egyptian education. If so, it must have helped him in writing poems to the One True God, the God of Israel.

The Hebrews used sacred songs. Miriam, Moses's sister, broke forth into song to celebrate the deliverance of Israel from the Egyptians when they were on the shore of the Red Sea. During the period of the Judges, the Bible records songs of Deborah. The boy David gave us the largest number of praise hymns, a collection of Psalms, which is considered the song book of the Bible. These Hebrew songs outranked those of all other nations.

In the New Testament period Mary sang the Magnificat (Luke 1:46-55) at the time the angel spoke to her of Jesus' birth to come. At the time of the birth the angels sang. Zechariah sang the Benedictus (Luke 1:67-79). Jesus must have heard much music when he was a boy. A large choir of Levites led the worshipers in the temple. Each day of the week certain Psalms were sung with the accompaniment of priests playing trumpets. Jesus was taught to sing the Psalms. The hymn sung at the Last Supper was probably Psalm 115.

After the ascension of Christ, his followers were persecuted so they hid in caves and sang as their number increased. Since they had to be careful to keep their meetings secret, we don't have a record of what they sang. Pliny, a Roman historian, wrote a letter to the Emperor about this time in which he informed him that the Christians would meet and offer praise to Christ as God.

Gradually the persecution lessened and more hymns were written. We sing a translation of "Shepherd of Tender Youth" written by Clement of Alexandria about 220 A.D.

An early Christian martyr who became the patron saint of church music was Cecilia. The date of her death, according to some, was 176 and others, 230. Excavations were made beneath the church where it is believed she was put to death in a small bath. In 1584 when the Academy of Music at Rome was founded, Cecilia was made its patroness and a church in Rome was named for her. She has been painted by artists and praised in literature through the ages.

About 300 years after Christ, the Council of Laodicea decreed that "besides the appointed singers, others shall not sing in the church." Therefore hymnody declined in the eastern church as it became liturgical. An exception was Bishop John Chrysostom who organized special processions of orthodox hymn singers. In 386 Ambrose of Milan began hymn singing in western churches. He developed the meter from the marching rhythm of the soldiers during some religious wars. There are 100 hymns attributed to him. One is "O Splendor of God's Glory Bright."

In the early 400s Prudentius was called the first truly Christian poet. His most popular hymn to survive is "Of the Father's Love Begotten." It is based on Revelation 1:8, which shows Christ as the "Alpha" (beginning) and "Omega" (end).

In the 500s an outstanding church leader was Pope Gregory I, called "the Great" because he was proficient in administration, missions, writing, preaching and especially in liturgy and music. He wrote the morning hymn "Father, We Praise You." Once during a plague he left his monastery (unusual at that time) and formed a musical procession to give comforting peace to the sick and dying. We now have the Gregorian chant from his book of chants published in 600.

Around 750 A.D. John of Damascus urged the use of pictures or images in the church and wrote hymns. In the time of the early Roman Empire, the Christian Church used the Greek language. Therefore during this period many Greek hymns were written in monasteries, later translated into Latin — and in the nineteenth century into English. John of Damascus wrote "Come, Ye Faithful, Raise the Strain" for St. Thomas Sunday, "The Day is Past and Over," and "The Day of Resurrection," which is traditionally sung in the Greek churches at midnight on Easter morning. After being given a signal, the people light candles all at once to give a sudden blaze of light. The hymn was written at the Mar Saba monastery overlooking the Dead Sea.

Theodulph was a poetic genius of the early 800s remembered for the hymn "All Glory, Laud, and Honor," written while he was a prisoner of King Louis I. It is a Palm Sunday hymn of the triumphal entry into Jerusalem (Mark 11:1-10 and John 12:12-19).

The Roman Catholic Church was the most powerful during the Middle Ages, so for 1,000 years hymns were written in Latin, the language of the church. One of the writers of the 1100s was Bernard of Clairvaux (1090-1153) who wrote "Jesus, the Very Thought of Thee." He was the most outstanding religious leader of that time. However, the English hymnologist Erik Routley says that it is possible the hymn may have been written by a French nun, anonymously.

Francis of Assisi, in the early 1200s, is known as "God's Troubadour." He wrote the famous "Canticle to the Sun." We know it as "All Creatures of Our God and King."

In Germany during the 1300s a more free, folksy kind of devotional expression was known as "carols." An example is "Good Christian Men (Friends), Rejoice." These combined the Latin of the church with the vernacular of the people. When the Catholic Church discouraged its members from singing in church, they sang outside the church at festivals and many other occasions.

In the sixteenth century (1500s) Martin Luther led the Protestant Reformation, against the wishes of the Roman Church. According to the church laws, only the priests could read from the Bible and perform the church music. As a result of the Reformation, Luther gave everyone opportunity to use the Bible and the hymn book. He translated them from Latin to German, their own language. Luther said he did this "so that God might speak directly to them in His Word and that they might answer Him in their songs."

Luther's 37 hymns were a great help in spreading his teaching, even though singing them was cause for imprisonment. There were 20,000 hymns written in Germany by the end of the sixteenth century, more than in any other country. Katherine Zell, a Lutheran minister's wife, who lived at the time of Luther, compiled hymn books for lay people. She describes her motivation: "When I read those hymns I felt that the writer had the whole Bible in his heart. This is not just a hymn book but a lesson book of prayer and praise." Her words could have been written today. "When so many filthy songs are on the lips of men and women and even children I think it well that folk should with lusty zeal and clear voice sing the songs of their salvation." She continues to explain why music is so important. "God is glad when the craftsman at his bench, the maid at the sink, the farmer at the plough, the dresser at the vines, the mother at the cradle break forth in hymns of prayer, praise and instruction."

Meanwhile, in France, Clement Marot translated the Psalms, which were sung to ballad tunes. As a result, he was excommunicated from the Catholic Church in France. He went to Geneva, Switzerland, where he published the popular *Geneva Psalter* in 1543. It was translated into many languages and has been the most used book of praise. Included in the book were metrical (rhythmic) Psalms sung in unison (soprano) with no harmony or instrumentation. Some people in Holland today will sing nothing else, so the Netherlands Reformed Church hymnals still have the Psalter. It has recently been included in other hymnals.

America entered the picture in the early 1600s. The Pilgrims brought with them from Holland the English Geneva Bible of 1560 which included, of course, the Psalms. When they first landed, Governor Bradford wrote that "they fell on their knees and blessed the God of heaven." The first book printed in America in 1640 was a Psalm book they used for worship and personal devotions called the *Bay Psalmist*. Psalm singing was useful in many ways. In colonial America very few people had clocks, so they timed their boiling of eggs by singing an eight-line verse of a Psalm.

In England, Isaac Watts (1674-1748) was called the "Father of English Hymnody" with his nearly 700 hymns. He began by paraphrasing Psalms, which led to writing his own original texts. Watts added harmony (alto, tenor and bass parts) to the soprano as well as instruments, usually organ.

The 1700s brought another renewal movement to England which spilled over into America led by brothers John and Charles Wesley. They both were clergymen in the Church of England, kept their membership there, but were itinerant preachers of a more personal experience with Christ which finally led to the founding of the Methodist denomination. Charles Wesley (1707-1788) specialized in writing hymns, numbering 7,000 or more. Many are considered our favorite hymns. A woman who helped with the Wesley movement was Selena, countess of Huntingdon. Along with her gifts of money to build 60 or more English chapels, she compiled *A Select Collection of Hymns*. The authors' names were not printed, so we don't know if she wrote any of them.

Due to the renewals and revivals which took place in the 1800s more laypeople were inspired to write hymns for publication. An example is Joseph Scriven who wrote "What a Friend We Have in Jesus." A number of women wrote hymns which became popular. English women writers were: Frances Havergal who wrote "Take My Life," Charlotte Elliott who wrote "Just As I Am," and Sarah Adams who wrote "Nearer,

My God, to Thee." In America the most prolific of hymn writers ever was Fanny Crosby, the blind woman who wrote "Blessed Assurance" and over 8,000 others.

In our twentieth century it will remain to be seen what sacred music will last. We do know that we all need to express our deep Christian love, gratitude, and praise to God through poetry and music, a universal language.

# Bibliography

Bailey, Albert Edward. *The Gospel in Hymns*. New York: Scribner. 1950.

Benson, Louis. The *English Hymn: Its Development and Use in Worship*. Philadelphia: The Presbyterian Board of Publication. 1915.

Benson, Louis. *Studies of Familiar Hymns: First Series*. Philadelphia: The Westminster Press. 1926 (c. 1903).

Benson, Louis. *Studies of Familiar Hymns: Second Series*. Philadelphia: The Westminster Press. 1923.

Bonner, Clint. *A Hymn is Born*. Chicago: Wilcox and Follett Company. 1952.

Clarkson, Margaret. *A Singing Heart*. Carol Stream, IL: Hope Publishing Company. 1987.

Claghorn, Gene. *Women Composers and Hymnists*. Meluchen, NJ: The Scarecrow Press. 1984.

*Dictionary of National Biography*, s.v. "Adams, Sarah Flower."

Hustad, Donald. *Dictionary Handbook to Hymns for the Church*. Carol Stream, IL: Hope Publishing Company. 1978.

Idle, Christopher. *Stories of Our Favorite Hymns*. Grand Rapids, MI: Eerdmans. 1980.

Johnson, Guy. *Treasury of Great Hymns and Their Stories*. Greenville, SC: Bob Jones University Press. 1986.

Julian, John. *A Dictionary of Hymnology*. New York: Scribner's Sons. 1891.

McCutchan, Robert. *Our Hymnody*. New York: Abingdon-Cokesbury Press. 1937.

Macmillan, D. *The Life of George Matheson*. New York: A. C. Armstrong and Son. 1907.

*The National Cyclopedia of American Biography*, s.v. "Howe, Julia Ward."

Osbeck, Kenneth W. *101 Hymn Stories*. Grand Rapids: Kregel Publications. 1982.

Osbeck, Kenneth W. *101 More Hymn Stories*. Grand Rapids: Kregel Publications. 1985.

Pollock, John. *Amazing Grace*. San Francisco: Harper and Row. 1981.

Price, Carl. *One Hundred and One Hymn Stories*. New York: The Abingdon Press. 1923.

Routley, Erik. *Christian Hymns Observed*. Princeton, NJ: Prestige Publications. 1982.

Smith, H. Augustine. *Lyric Religion*. New York: D. Appleton-Century Company. 1931.

Spencer, Donald A. *Hymn and Scripture Selection Guide*. Grand Rapids: Baker Book House. 1993.

Stebbins, George C. *Reminiscences and Gospel Hymn Stories*. New York: George H. Doran Company. 1924.

Young, Carlton R. *Companion to the United Methodist Hymnal*. Nashville: Abingdon Press. 1993.

# Index